A Year of Amigurumi Friends

24 PATTERNS FOR CUTE CROCHET ANIMALS

Andreia Ferreira

DAVID & CHARLES
—PUBLISHING—

www.davidandcharles.com

CONTENTS

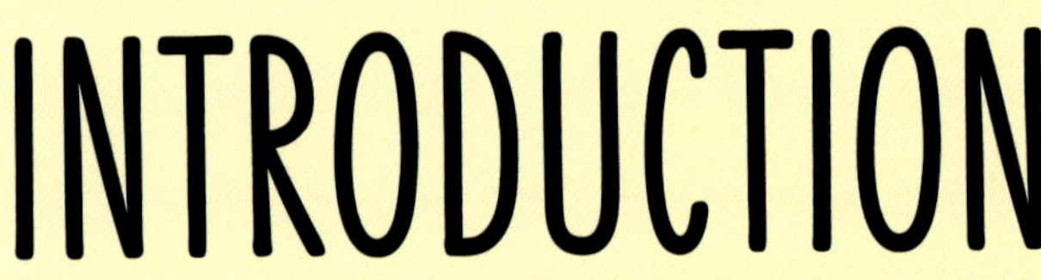

INTRODUCTION

Welcome to A Year of Amigurumi Friends!

In this book, you'll be introduced to 24 adorable characters that pair up for each month, bringing with them unique stories, which will keep your hands busy all year long. You'll be able to enjoy a romantic date in February with Dash and Dawn the Deers, spend the hot summer days of July by the beach with Gia the Giraffe and Rory the Rhino, and even celebrate Christmas with Riley the Reindeer and Mason the Mouse.

The concept for this book started brewing in the back of my mind in January 2020. I've always enjoyed designing characters representing nature and holidays, so I knew that one day I would be making a collection of designs about it. Unfortunately, and mostly because of lack of time, my sketches remained just ideas for potential characters. Or so I thought.

Fast track to 2023, when I decided to pick up this concept again. With the support and encouragement of my Patreon community, I revisited my early sketches and designed two amigurumi friends every month for a whole year. It was a year of hard work that ultimately paid off in the best possible way.

This book is the culmination of what I've learned over the years as a designer, but it's also a representation of who I am as a person. Wonder why April features amigurumi friends inspired by birthday parties? April baby over here! Or why do the amigurumi friends in June travel to Switzerland and Japan? I was born in Switzerland and my dream travel destination has always been Japan, which I was lucky enough to visit on my honeymoon.

I hope all these amigurumi friends (the old and the new) will bring you as much joy and inspiration as they did for me. Now it's time to pick up your crochet hook and get your hands working!

Love,

Andreia

GETTING STARTED

Abbreviations

BLO back loop only
ch chain
cont continu(e)ing
dc double crochet
dec work 2 single crochet stitches together (decrease 1 st)
sc3tog work 3 single crochet stitches together (decrease 2 sts)
FLO front loop only
hdc half double crochet
inc work 2 single crochet stitches in the next stitch (increase 1 st)
PM place marker
rep repeat
rnd(s) round(s)
RS right side
sc single crochet
slst slip stitch
sp(s) space(s)
st(s) stitch(es)

Pattern difficulty levels

The patterns in this book are rated as Easy (X), Intermediate (X X), or Advanced (X X X). The rating system is based on how the characters work as a collection and may differ from the standard crochet rating system.

Easy: A project of this level will have simple shapes and basic stitches and may include one special stitch explained in the Techniques section. These projects require less time to complete.

Intermediate: A project of this level will have a balance of simple and intricate shaping and may include multiple color changes and special stitches.

Advanced: A project of this level will have multiple color changes, a fair amount of pieces to assemble, and intricate shaping either in the character or accessories. These projects require the most time to complete.

US/UK terminology conversions

The patterns are written in US terminology. For the equivalent UK terms, see below.

US	UK
Single crochet (sc)	Double crochet (dc)
Half double crochet (hdc)	Half treble crochet (htr)
Double crochet (dc)	Treble crochet (tr)
Yarn over hook (yoh)	Yarn round hook (yrh)
skip	miss

TOOLS & MATERIALS

Yarn

I used Hobbii Friends Cotton 8/4, a fingering (4-ply) yarn, for all the projects in this book. I prefer working with cotton because of the stitch definition it creates, and how sturdy the fabric is for amigurumi.

For each project, a list of the shades used is provided but not the exact yarn quantities. You will only need small amounts, or at most one ball of yarn for each color will be enough. Using a different fiber or even a different yarn weight is possible, but then the proportions of your amigurumi won't be the same as the dimensions listed.

Crochet hook

The size of the crochet hook you will use may vary depending on your preference and gauge/tension (how tight your stitches are). My favorite crochet hooks are from Tulip, especially the Etimo Red and Etimo Rose. I used a 2.20mm crochet hook, which doesn't have a direct correspondence to US sizing — the closest one being the 2.25mm (US/B1) crochet hook.

Other tools and materials

Besides the yarn and crochet hook, other things may be useful for amigurumi making.

TOY SAFETY EYES

I used plain black safety eyes in different sizes — or, in some cases, I embroidered the eyes — but there are many different types that you could use to give different personalities to the characters. Just remember: if gifting these toys to small children embroidery is more suitable for safety concerns.

TOY STUFFING

Amigurumi need to be stuffed, and polyester fiberfill will do the job. Make sure to stuff your amigurumi firmly so they can hold their shape. You can even use a wooden skewer to help you compact the stuffing and reach small spaces when needed.

STITCH MARKERS

Stitch markers are very useful to keep track of your rounds, but also help identify other important stitches throughout. You can use any type of removable stitch marker or even a scrap of contrasting yarn.

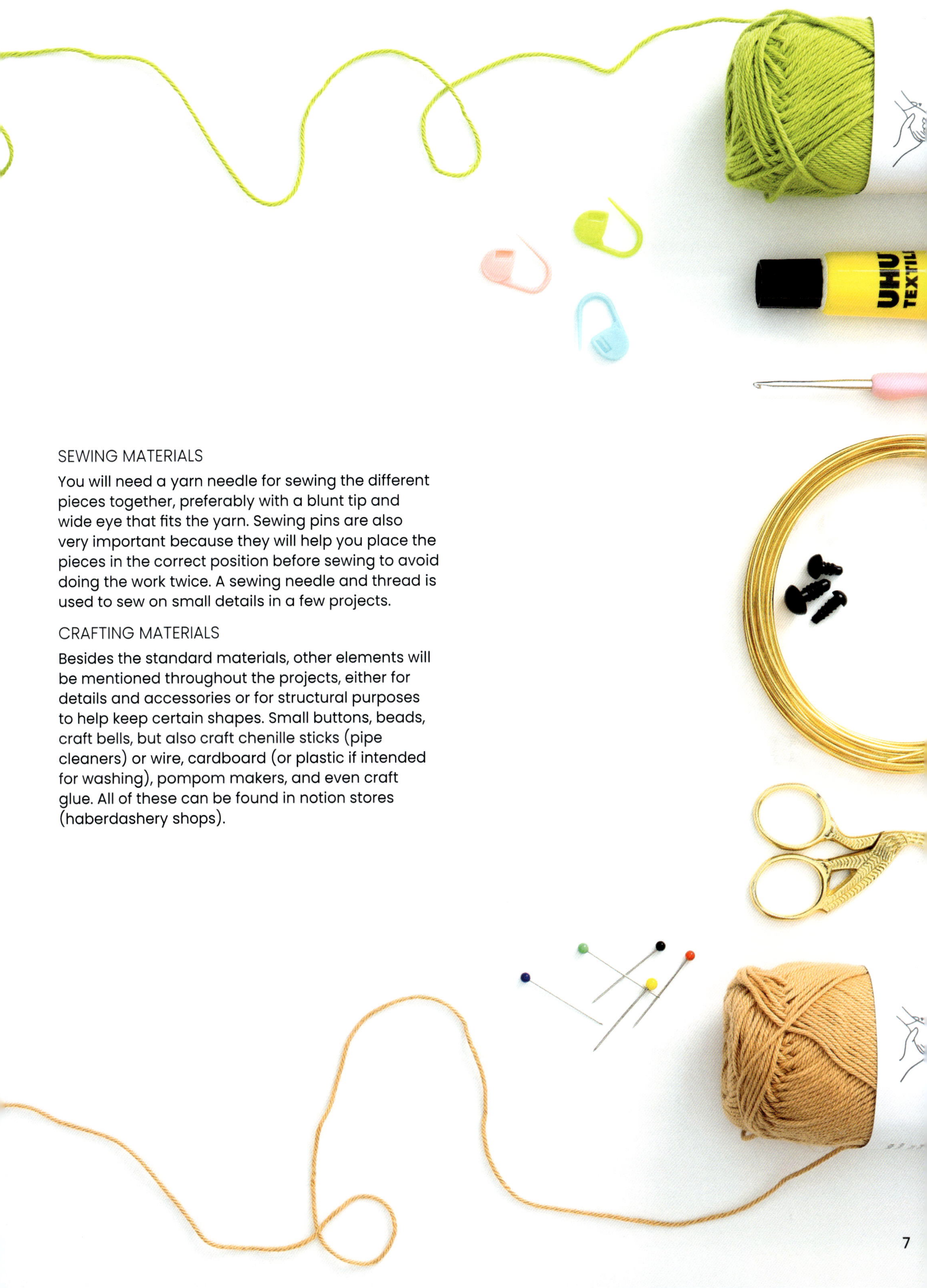

SEWING MATERIALS

You will need a yarn needle for sewing the different pieces together, preferably with a blunt tip and wide eye that fits the yarn. Sewing pins are also very important because they will help you place the pieces in the correct position before sewing to avoid doing the work twice. A sewing needle and thread is used to sew on small details in a few projects.

CRAFTING MATERIALS

Besides the standard materials, other elements will be mentioned throughout the projects, either for details and accessories or for structural purposes to help keep certain shapes. Small buttons, beads, craft bells, but also craft chenille sticks (pipe cleaners) or wire, cardboard (or plastic if intended for washing), pompom makers, and even craft glue. All of these can be found in notion stores (haberdashery shops).

JANUARY

Poppy Penguin & Wilbur Walrus

Every year, during the peak winter season of the Northern Hemisphere, Poppy leaves the South Pole to meet with her best friend Wilbur on the other side of the world. They first met during an exchange program and their friendship grew from there. Wilbur always looks forward to meeting Poppy and makes sure to have delicious fish snacks ready for when she arrives.

POPPY 13CM (5 1/8IN) WILBUR 12.5CM (5IN)

PATTERN NOTES

Most pieces are worked in a spiral without joining each round with a slst. The ear muff band and the beanie are worked in rows.

YOU WILL NEED

YARNS:

Hobbii Friends Cotton 8/4 (100% cotton) fingering (4-ply) weight, 160m (174yd) per 50g (1¾oz) ball, in the following shades:

FOR BOTH

- ✓ **Pale Pink:** 1 ball in Rose (44)
- ✓ **Red:** 1 ball in Tomato (40)
- ✓ **Light Blue:** 1 ball in Icy Blue (76)
- ✓ **Deep Blue:** 1 ball in French Blue (84)
- ✓ **White:** 1 ball in White (01)

FOR POPPY

- ✓ **Dark Gray:** 1 ball in Charcoal (123)
- ✓ **Dark Yellow:** 1 ball in Dark Yellow (26)

FOR WILBUR

- ✓ **Brown:** 1 ball in Cappuccino (10)
- ✓ **Cream:** 1 ball in Oatmilk (03)

HOOK:

- ✓ 2.20mm (US B/1) crochet hook

TOOLS AND MATERIALS:

- ✓ 2 pairs of 8mm safety eyes
- ✓ Stitch markers
- ✓ Yarn needle
- ✓ Toy stuffing
- ✓ Sewing needle and black embroidery floss (thread)

Poppy

Head

Rnd 1: using Dark Gray, sc 6 in a magic ring. (6 sts)

Rnd 2: inc 6 times. (12 sts)

Rnd 3: [sc 1, inc] 6 times. (18 sts)

Rnd 4: [sc 2, inc] 6 times. (24 sts)

Rnd 5: [sc 3, inc] 6 times. (30 sts)

Rnd 6: [sc 4, inc] 6 times. (36 sts)

Rnd 7: [sc 5, inc] 6 times. (42 sts)

Rnd 8: [sc 6, inc] 6 times. (48 sts)

Rnd 9: sc 1 in each st.

Cont alternating from Dark Gray to White to make face patch.

Rnd 10: (Dark Gray) sc 16, (White) sc 4, (Dark Gray) sc 8, (White) sc 4, (Dark Gray) sc 16. (48 sts)

Rnd 11: (Dark Gray) sc 15, (White) sc 6, (Dark Gray) sc 6, (White) sc 6, (Dark Gray) sc 15. (48 sts)

Rnds 12 and 13 (2 rnds): (Dark Gray) sc 14, (White) sc 7, (Dark Gray) sc 6, (White) sc 7, (Dark Gray) sc 14. (48 sts)

Rnd 14: (Dark Gray) sc 7, inc, sc 6, (White) sc 1, inc, sc 5, (Dark Gray) sc 2, inc, sc 3, (White) sc 4, inc, sc 2, (Dark Gray) sc 5, inc, sc 7, inc. (54 sts)

Rnds 15–19 (5 rnds): (Dark Gray) sc 15, (White) sc 23, (Dark Gray) sc 16. (54 sts)

Rnd 20: (Dark Gray) sc 7, dec, sc 6, (White) sc 1, dec, [sc 7, dec] twice, sc 2, (Dark Gray) sc 5, dec, sc 7, dec. (48 sts)

Rnd 21: (Dark Gray) sc 6, dec, sc 6, (White) dec, [sc 6, dec] twice, sc 2, (Dark Gray) sc 4, dec, sc 6, dec. (42 sts)

Rnd 22: (Dark Gray) sc 5, dec, sc 7, (White) dec, sc 3, dec, sc 5, dec, sc 1, (Dark Gray) sc 4, dec, sc 5, dec. (36 sts)

Cont working in Dark Gray only.

Place safety eyes on face patch between Rnds 14 and 15, 11 sts apart.

Start stuffing, cont as you work.

Rnd 23: [sc 4, dec] 6 times. (30 sts)

Rnd 24: [sc 3, dec] 6 times. (24 sts)

Rnd 25: [sc 2, dec] 6 times. (18 sts)

Rnd 26: [sc 1, dec] 6 times. (12 sts)

Rnd 27: dec 6 times. (6 sts)

Fasten off, sew hole closed by pulling yarn tail through front loops of remaining sts.

Beak

Rnd 1: using Dark Yellow, ch 8, start in 2nd ch from hook working in back bump of ch, sc 6, sc 3 in last ch, turn, cont on other side of ch (see Techniques: Crocheting Around Foundation Chain) working through both loops, sc 5, inc in last ch. (16 sts)

Rnds 2 and 3 (2 rnds): sc 1 in each st.

Fasten off, leaving long tail for sewing.

Do not stuff. Sew beak to the head centered with eyes on Rnds 15 and 16.

Cheeks (make 2)

Rnd 1: using Pale Pink, sc 6 in a magic ring. (6 sts)

Rnd 2: inc 6 times. (12 sts)

Fasten off invisibly, leaving long tail for sewing (see Techniques: Invisible Fasten Off).

Sew cheeks next to eyes between Rnds 15 and 18.

Legs and body

LEG 1

Rnd 1: using Dark Gray, sc 6 in a magic ring. (6 sts)

Rnd 2: inc 6 times. (12 sts)

Rnd 3: [sc 3, inc] 3 times. (15 sts)

Rnd 4: sc 1 in each st.

Rnd 5: [sc 2, inc, sc 2] 3 times. (18 sts)

Fasten off. Set aside.

LEG 2

Work as for leg 1, but do not fasten off at end. Cont working on body.

BODY

Rnd 6: still with leg 2 on hook, ch 1, sc 1 in last st of leg 1 to join (see Techniques: Joining Legs), PM here for new beg of rnd, sc 1 in each st of leg 1, inc on ch, sc 1 in each st of leg 2, inc on ch. (40 sts)

Stuff legs firmly.

Rnd 7: [sc 9, inc] 4 times. (44 sts)

Rnds 8–11 (4 rnds): sc 1 in each st.

1	2	3
New Year's Day		

Rnd 12: change to Red, slst 1 in each st loosely.

Rnd 13: working in BLO of Rnd 12 and both loops of Rnd 11 (see Techniques: Straight Stripe Color Change), sc 1 in each st.

Rnd 14: change to White, sc 1 in each st.

Rnd 15: change to Red, [sc 20, dec] twice. (42 sts)

Rnd 16: sc 1 in each st.

Cont alternating from Red to White to make sweater pattern.

Rnd 17: [(Red) sc 1, (White) sc 1, (Red) sc 1, (White) sc 1, (Red) sc 2] 7 times. (42 sts)

Rnd 18: [(White) sc 2, (Red) sc 1, (White) sc 2, (Red) sc 1] 7 times. (42 sts)

Rnd 19: (Red) sc 1 in each st.

Rnd 20: rep Rnd 18.

Rnd 21: rep Rnd 17.

Cont working in Red only.

Rnd 22: sc 5, dec, sc 15, dec, sc 10, dec, sc 6. (39 sts)

Rnd 23: sc 1 in each st.

Rnd 24: change to White, [sc 11, dec] 3 times. (36 sts)

Rnd 25: change to Red, sc 1 in each st.

Rnd 26: [sc 5, dec, sc 5] 3 times. (33 sts)

Rnd 27: [sc 9, dec] 3 times. (30 sts)

Rnd 28: work in BLO, [sc 3, dec] 6 times. (24 sts)

Fasten off, leaving long tail for sewing. Stuff body firmly.

SWEATER COLLAR DETAIL

Hold body up and join Red to first unworked loop of Rnd 27 (see Techniques: Joining Yarn to Add a Detail) with slst 1 (does not count as a st). Start next rnd in same st.

Rnd 1: ch 2, hdc 1 in each st, slst 1 to first st to join. (30 sts)

Fasten off and weave in yarn ends.

SWEATER HEM DETAIL

Hold body with legs up and join Red to first unworked loop of Rnd 12 with slst 1 (does not count as a st). Start next rnd in same st.

Rnd 1: sc 1 in each st. (44 sts)

Fasten off invisibly and weave in yarn ends

Feet (make 2)

Rnd 1: using Dark Yellow, sc 6 in a magic ring. (6 sts)

Rnd 2: inc 6 times. (12 sts)

Rnd 3: sc 1 in each st.

Rnd 4: [sc 5, inc] twice. (14 sts)

Rnds 5 and 6 (2 rnds): sc 1 in each st.

Do not stuff. Flatten opening and work next row through both layers to close (see Techniques: Closing with Single Crochet).

Row 7: sc 1, [hdc 3 in same st, slst 1] twice, hdc 3 in same st, sc 1. (13 sts)

Fasten off, leaving long tail for sewing.

Bring yarn tail to top of foot between Rnds 3 and 4 (see Photo 1). Sew feet to bottom of legs (see Photo 2).

Arms (make 2)

Rnd 1: using Dark Gray, sc 6 in a magic ring. (6 sts)

Rnd 2: [sc 1, inc] 3 times. (9 sts)

Rnd 3: [sc 1, inc, sc 1] 3 times. (12 sts)

Rnd 4: [sc 3, inc] 3 times. (15 sts)

Rnds 5 and 6 (2 rnds): sc 1 in each st.

Rnd 7: change to Red, slst 1 in each st loosely.

Rnd 8: working in BLO of Rnd 7 and both loops of Rnd 6, sc 1 in each st.

Rnds 9–13 (5 rnds): sc 1 in each st.

Rnd 14: [sc 3, dec] 3 times. (12 sts)

Rnds 15–17 (3 rnds): sc 1 in each st.

Do not stuff. Flatten opening and work next row through both layers to close.

Row 18: sc 6. (6 sts)

Fasten off, leaving long tail for sewing.

SWEATER CUFF DETAIL

Hold arm with hand up and join Red to first unworked loop of Rnd 7 with slst 1 (does not count as a st). Start next rnd in same st.

Rnd 1: sc 1 in each st. (15 sts)

Fasten off invisibly and weave in yarn ends.

Sew arms on each side of body between Rnds 26 and 27.

Tail

Rnd 1: using Dark Gray, sc 6 in a magic ring. (6 sts)

Rnd 2: [sc 1, inc] 3 times. (9 sts)

Rnd 3: sc 1 in each st.

Fasten off, leaving long tail for sewing.

Do not stuff. Sew tail to back of body on Rnds 8 and 9 (see Photo 3).

Ear muffs

Start by making cups and band separately.

CUPS (MAKE 2)

Rnd 1: using Light Blue, sc 6 in a magic ring. (6 sts)

Rnd 2: inc 6 times. (12 sts)

Rnd 3: [sc 1, inc] 6 times. (18 sts)

Rnds 4 and 5 (2 rnds): sc 1 in each st.

Rnd 6: change to Deep Blue, work in FLO, hdc 1 in each st.

Fasten off Light Blue, leaving long tail for sewing. Fasten off Deep Blue invisibly and weave in yarn ends.

BAND

Leave long tail at beginning of chain for sewing.

Row 1: using Deep Blue, ch 25, start in 2nd ch from hook working in back bump of ch, sc 24, turn. (24 sts)

Row 2: ch 1, sc 24. (24 sts)

Fasten off, leaving long tail for sewing.

Sew ends of band to each cup (see Photo 4).

Place ear muffs over head and sew cups on each side of head using unworked loops from Rnd 5. Stuff cups as you sew (see Photo 5).

Wilbur

Head and body

Rnd 1: using Brown, sc 6 in a magic ring. (6 sts)

Rnd 2: inc 6 times. (12 sts)

Rnd 3: [sc 1, inc] 6 times. (18 sts)

Rnd 4: [sc 2, inc] 6 times. (24 sts)

Rnd 5: [sc 3, inc] 6 times. (30 sts)

Rnd 6: [sc 4, inc] 6 times. (36 sts)

Rnd 7: [sc 5, inc] 6 times. (42 sts)

Rnd 8: [sc 6, inc] 6 times. (48 sts)

Rnd 9: [sc 15, inc] 3 times. (51 sts)

Rnd 10: [sc 8, inc, sc 8] 3 times. (54 sts)

Rnds 11–18 (8 rnds): sc 1 in each st.

Rnd 19: [sc 17, inc] 3 times. (57 sts)

Rnds 20 and 21 (2 rnds): sc 1 in each st.

Rnd 22: [sc 9, inc, sc 9] 3 times. (60 sts)

Rnd 23: change to Deep Blue, slst 1 in each st loosely.

Rnd 24: working in BLO of Rnd 23 and both loops of Rnd 22 (see Techniques: Straight Stripe Color Change), sc 1 in each st.

Rnd 25: change to White, [sc 19, inc] 3 times. (63 sts)

Rnd 26: change to Deep Blue, sc 1 in each st.

Rnd 27: change to White, [sc 10, inc, sc 10] 3 times. (66 sts)

Rnd 28: change to Deep Blue, sc 1 in each st.

Rnd 29: change to White, [sc 21, inc] 3 times. (69 sts)

Rnd 30: change to Deep Blue, [sc 11, inc, sc 11] 3 times. (72 sts)

Rnd 31: change to White, sc 1 in each st.

Rnd 32: change to Deep Blue, sc 12, inc, sc 45, inc, sc 12, inc. (75 sts)

Rnd 33: change to White, sc 1 in each st.

Rnd 34: change to Deep Blue, sc 12, inc, sc 48, inc, sc 12, inc. (78 sts)

Rnd 35: change to Brown, work in BLO, sc 1 in each st.

Rnd 36: sc 12, inc, sc 51, inc, sc 12, inc. (81 sts)

Place safety eyes between Rnds 14 and 15, 10 sts apart Make sure eyes are opposite increases on back of body.

Start stuffing, cont as you work.

Rnds 37–40 (4 rnds): sc 1 in each st.

Rnd 41: [sc 7, dec] 9 times. (72 sts)

Rnd 42: [sc 10, dec] 6 times. (66 sts)

Rnd 43: [sc 9, dec] 6 times. (60 sts)

Rnd 44: [sc 8, dec] 6 times. (54 sts)

Rnd 45: [sc 7, dec] 6 times. (48 sts)

Rnd 46: [sc 6, dec] 6 times. (42 sts)

Rnd 47: [sc 5, dec] 6 times. (36 sts)

Rnd 48: [sc 4, dec] 6 times. (30 sts)

Stuff body firmly until this point only to create a flat bottom.

Rnd 49: [sc 3, dec] 6 times. (24 sts)

Rnd 50: [sc 2, dec] 6 times. (18 sts)

Rnd 51: [sc 1, dec] 6 times. (12 sts)

Rnd 52: dec 6 times. (6 sts)

Fasten off, sew hole closed by pulling yarn tail through front loops of remaining sts.

SHIRT COLLAR DETAIL

Hold body up and join Deep Blue (see Techniques: Joining Yarn to Add a Detail) to first unworked loop of Rnd 23 with slst 1 (counts as first st of next rnd).

Rnd 1: slst 1 in each st. (60 sts)

Fasten off invisibly and weave in yarn ends (see Techniques: Invisible Fasten Off).

SHIRT HEM DETAIL

Hold body upside down and join Deep Blue to first unworked loop of Rnd 34 with slst 1 (counts as first st of next rnd).

Rnd 1: slst 1 in each st. (78 sts)

Fasten off invisibly and weave in yarn ends.

Tusks (make 2)

Rnd 1: using White, sc 6 in a magic ring. (6 sts)

Rnd 2: [sc 2, inc] twice. (8 sts)

Rnds 3–6 (4 rnds): sc 1 in each st.

Fasten off, leaving long tail for sewing.

Stuff firmly.

Snout

Start by making the bumps.

BUMPS (MAKE 2)

Rnd 1: using Cream, sc 6 in a magic ring. (6 sts)

Rnd 2: inc 6 times. (12 sts)

Rnd 3: sc 1 in each st.

Fasten off first bump leaving long tail for sewing. Do not fasten off 2nd bump.

JOINING THE BUMPS

Rnd 4: still with 2nd bump on hook, sc 1 in first st of first bump to join, PM here for new beg of rnd, sc 1 in each st of first bump, sc 1 in each st of 2nd bump. (24 sts)

Use yarn tail of first bump to sew gap between bumps.

Rnd 5: sc 1 in each st.

Rnd 6: [sc 2, dec] 6 times. (18 sts)

Rnd 7: [sc 1, dec] 6 times. (12 sts)

Stuff firmly.

Rnd 8: dec 6 times. (6 sts)

Fasten off, leaving long tail for sewing, sew hole closed by pulling yarn tail through front loops of remaining sts.

Using Brown, embroider nose on snout using straight stitch (see Techniques: Straight Stitch). Make 6 horizontal lines between Rnds 6 and 7 that are 3 sts wide, centered with gap between bumps.

Sew tusks to bottom of each bump of snout.

Sew the snout centered with eyes between Rnds 14 and 17.

Cheeks (make 2)

Rnd 1: using Pale Pink, sc 6 in a magic ring. (6 sts)

Rnd 2: inc 6 times. (12 sts)

Fasten off invisibly, leaving long tail for sewing.

Sew cheeks next to eyes between Rnds 15 and 18.

Tail

Start by making hind flippers.

HIND FLIPPERS (MAKE 2)

Rnd 1: using Brown, sc 6 in a magic ring. (6 sts)

Rnd 2: [sc 1, inc] 3 times. (9 sts)

Rnd 3: sc 1 in each st.

Rnd 4: sc 3, inc twice, sc 4. (11 sts)

Rnd 5: sc 1 in each st.

Rnd 6: sc 4, inc twice, sc 5. (13 sts)

Rnd 7: sc 1 in each st.

Rnd 8: sc 5, inc twice, sc 6. (15 sts)

Rnd 9: sc 1 in each st.

Rnd 10: sc 5, dec twice, sc 4, dec. (12 sts)

Fasten off first hind flipper, leaving long tail for sewing. Do not fasten off 2nd hind flipper.

Do not stuff.

JOINING THE HIND FLIPPERS

Rnd 11: sc 7, end rnd here. (7 sts)

Rnd 12: still with 2nd hind flipper on hook, sc 1 in 7th st of first hind flipper to join, PM here for new beg of rnd, sc 1 in each st of first hind flipper, sc 1 in each st of 2nd hind flipper. (24 sts)

Use yarn tail of first hind flipper to sew gap between hind flippers.

Rnd 13: sc 6, [sc 1, inc] 3 times, [inc, sc 1] 3 times, sc 6. (30 sts)

Rnds 14 and 15 (2 rnds): sc 1 in each st.

Rnd 16: sc 6, [sc 1, inc, sc 1] 6 times, sc 6. (36 sts)

Rnds 17 and 18 (2 rnds): sc 1 in each st.

Rnd 19: sc 6, [sc 1, inc, sc 2] 3 times, [sc 2, inc, sc 1] 3 times, sc 6. (42 sts)

Rnd 20: sc 1 in each st.

Fasten off, leaving long tail for sewing.

Stuff firmly. Sew tail to back of body between Rnds 37 and 46. Bottom of tail should lay flat on surface (see Photo 1).

Front flippers (make 2)

Rnd 1: using Brown, sc 6 in a magic ring. (6 sts)

Rnd 2: inc 6 times. (12 sts)

Rnd 3: [sc 1, inc] 6 times. (18 sts)

1

2

Rnd 4: [sc 5, inc] 3 times. (21 sts)

Rnds 5–10 (6 rnds): sc 1 in each st.

Rnd 11: [sc 5, dec] 3 times. (18 sts)

Rnds 12–17 (6 rnds): sc 1 in each st.

Rnd 18: [sc 4, dec] 3 times. (15 sts)

Rnd 19: sc 1 in each st.

Do not stuff. Flatten opening and work next row through both layers to close (see Techniques: Closing with Single Crochet).

Row 20: sc 7, leave 1 st unworked. (7 sts)

Fasten off, leaving long tail for sewing.

Using black embroidery floss, embroider an anchor on one front flipper (see Photo 2).

Sew front flippers on sides of body between Rnds 30 and 31, 20 sts apart at front. Tattooed front flipper should be on right. Secure middle of front flippers to body with a few sewn stitches.

Heart patch

Rnd 1: using Red, working in magic ring, ch 1, hdc 2, sc 1, ch 2, sc 1, hdc 2, ch 1, slst 1. (7 sts + 4 chs)

Fasten off, leaving long tail for sewing.

Sew heart patch to front of sweater on left side.

Beanie

Row 1: using Red, ch 22, start in 2nd ch from hook, sc 7, hdc 14, turn. (21 sts)

Row 2: ch 2, work in BLO, hdc 14, sc 7, turn.

Row 3: ch 1, work in BLO, sc 7, hdc 14, turn.

Rows 4–33 (30 rows): rep Rows 2 and 3 fifteen more times.

IF NECESSARY, ADJUST THE TOTAL NUMBER OF ROWS SO THE BEANIE FITS THE HEAD OF WILBUR THE WALRUS.

Fasten off, leaving long tail for sewing.

Sew last row of beanie to foundation chain to make a tube (see Photo 3). Then, sew top opening closed by threading needle up and down edge of top (see Photo 4). Pull yarn tail tightly to close opening and add a few extra sewn stitches if necessary.

Fold bottom of beanie up to make a brim. Place beanie on Wilbur the Walrus' head.

Fish snack

Rnd 1: using Light Blue, sc 5 in a magic ring. (5 sts)

Rnd 2: inc 5 times. (10 sts)

Rnd 3: sc 1 in each st.

Rnd 4: [sc 1, inc] 5 times. (15 sts)

Rnds 5–12 (8 rnds): sc 1 in each st.

Rnd 13: [sc 3, dec] 3 times. (12 sts)

Rnd 14: sc 1 in each st.

Rnd 15: [sc 2, dec] 3 times. (9 sts)

Do not stuff. Flatten opening and work next row through both layers to close.

Row 16: sc 4, turn, leaving 1 st unworked. (4 sts)

Row 17: [ch 5, start in 2nd ch from hook, slst 1, sc 1, hdc 1, sc 1, cont working on Row 16, skip 1 st, slst 1] twice. (2 fins)

Fasten off and weave in yarn ends.

Using White, embroider an "X" for eye on each side of fish snack (see Photo 5).

3

4

5

FEBRUARY

Dash & Dawn Deer

Romance is in the air and the cutest couple in the woods is ready for date night. Dash and Dawn the Deers love to dress in matching outfits for special occasions like this, and it looks like Dash even has a little gift for his girlfriend.

DASH 18CM (7IN)

DAWN 15.5CM (6IN)

PATTERN NOTES

Most pieces are worked in a spiral without joining each round. The muzzle piece for the cap, straps for the pants, skirt, and headband are all worked in rows.

DIFFICULTY LEVEL ☒☒☐

YOU WILL NEED

YARNS:

Hobbii Friends Cotton 8/4 (100% cotton) fingering (4-ply) weight, 160m (174yd) per 50g (1¾oz) ball, in the following shades:

FOR BOTH

- ✓ **Light Brown:** 1 ball in Nougat (09)
- ✓ **Cream:** 1 ball in Oatmilk (03)
- ✓ **Brown:** 1 ball in Cappuccino (10)
- ✓ **Pale Pink:** 1 ball in Rose (44)
- ✓ **Dark Pink:** 1 ball in Mulberry (55)
- ✓ **White:** 1 ball in White (01)

FOR DASH

- ✓ **Yellow Green:** small amount in Pistachio (108)

HOOK:

- ✓ 2.20mm (US B/1) crochet hook

TOOLS AND MATERIALS:

- ✓ 2 pairs of 8mm safety eyes
- ✓ Yarn needle
- ✓ Toy stuffing
- ✓ Stitch markers
- ✓ 2 small buttons
- ✓ Sewing needle and white thread
- ✓ Craft chenille stems (pipe cleaners) or craft wire

Dash

Head

Rnd 1: using Cream, sc 6 in a magic ring. (6 sts)

Rnd 2: inc in each st. (12 sts)

Rnd 3: [sc 1, inc] 6 times. (18 sts)

Rnd 4: [sc 2, inc] 6 times. (24 sts)

Rnd 5: [sc 3, inc] 6 times. (30 sts)

Rnd 6: [sc 4, inc] 6 times. (36 sts)

Rnd 7: [sc 5, inc] 6 times. (42 sts)

Rnd 8: [sc 6, inc] 6 times. (48 sts)

Rnd 9: [sc 15, inc] 3 times. (51 sts)

Rnds 10–12 (3 rnds): sc 1 in each st.

Rnd 13: [sc 16, inc] 3 times. (54 sts)

Rnd 14–21 (8 rnds): sc 1 in each st.

Rnd 22: [sc 7, dec] 6 times. (48 sts)

Rnd 23: [sc 6, dec] 6 times. (42 sts)

Rnd 24: [sc 5, dec] 6 times. (36 sts)

Place safety eyes between Rnds 15 and 16, 11 sts apart.

Start stuffing, cont as you work.

Rnd 25: [sc 4, dec] 6 times. (30 sts)

Rnd 26: [sc 3, dec] 6 times. (24 sts)

Rnd 27: [sc 2, dec] 6 times. (18 sts)

Rnd 28: [sc 1, dec] 6 times. (12 sts)

Rnd 29: dec 6 times. (6 sts)

Fasten off, sew hole closed by pulling yarn tail through front loops of remaining sts.

Muzzle

Rnd 1: using Cream, sc 6 in a magic ring. (6 sts)

Rnd 2: inc in each st. (12 sts)

Rnd 3: [sc 1, inc] 6 times. (18 sts)

Rnd 4: [sc 5, inc] 3 times. (21 sts)

Rnds 5–7 (3 rnds): sc 1 in each st.

Fasten off, leaving long tail for sewing.

Stuff firmly. Sew muzzle to teh head centered with eyes, between Rnds 16 and 21 (see Photo 1).

Cap

Start by making headpiece and muzzle piece of cap separately.

HEADPIECE

Rnd 1: using Light Brown, sc 6 in a magic ring. (6 sts)

Rnd 2: inc in each st. (12 sts)

Rnd 3: [sc 1, inc] 6 times. (18 sts)

Rnd 4: [sc 2, inc] 6 times. (24 sts)

Rnd 5: [sc 3, inc] 6 times. (30 sts)

Rnd 6: [sc 4, inc] 6 times. (36 sts)

Rnd 7: [sc 5, inc] 6 times. (42 sts)

Rnd 8: [sc 6, inc] 6 times. (48 sts)

Rnd 9: [sc 7, inc] 6 times. (54 sts)

Rnds 10–16 (7 rnds): sc 1 in each st.

Fasten off invisibly and weave in yarn end (see Techniques: Invisible Fasten Off).

MUZZLE PIECE OF CAP

Hold headpiece upside down and join Light Brown to 24th st of Rnd 16 with slst 1 (does not count as a st) (see Techniques: Joining Yarn to Add a Detail). Start next row in same st.

Rows 1–2 (2 rows): ch 1, sc 8, turn. (8 sts)

Row 3: ch 1, skip 1 st, sc 7, turn. (7 sts)

Row 4: ch 1, sc 7, turn. (7 sts)

Row 5: ch 1, sc 5, dec, turn. (6 sts)

Row 6: ch 1, sc 6, turn. (6 sts)

Row 7: ch 1, skip 1 st, sc 5, turn. (5 sts)

Row 8: ch 1, sc 5, turn. (5 sts)

Row 9: ch 1, sc 3, dec, turn. (4 sts)

Row 10: ch 1, sc 4, turn. (4 sts)

Row 11: ch 1, skip 1 st, sc 3, turn. (3 sts)

Row 12: ch 1, skip 1 st, sc 2, turn. (2 sts)

Row 13: ch 1, skip 1 st, sc 1. (1 st)

Cont working around headpiece and muzzle piece.

Rnd 14: working on side of rows, sc 12, working on Rnd 16, sc 46, working on side of rows, sc 12. (70 sts)

Fasten off invisibly, leaving long tail for sewing.

Place cap on head, with end of muzzle piece on Rnd 4 of muzzle, 6 sts above eyes (see Photos 1 and 2). Sew in place.

Using Brown, embroider nose on muzzle with straight stitch (see Techniques: Straight Stitch). Make 6 horizontal lines between Rnds 3 and 4, covering end of extended part of head cover. Then embroider a vertical stitch, 3 rnds tall centered with nose, and a side smile over Rnds 2 and 3.

Using Cream, embroider fur details on cap (see Photo 3).

Cheeks (make 2)

Rnd 1: using Pale Pink, sc 6 in a magic ring. (6 sts)

Rnd 2: inc in each st. (12 sts)

Fasten off invisibly, leaving long tail for sewing.

Sew cheeks next to eyes between Rnds 16 and 19.

Antlers (make 2)

Start by making tines of antlers.

SMALL TINES (MAKE 1 FOR EACH ANTLER)

Rnd 1: using Brown, sc 6 in a magic ring. (6 sts)

Rnds 2–4 (3 rnds): sc 1 in each st.

Fasten off and weave in yarn end. Set aside.

Stuff firmly.

LONG TINES (MAKE 1 FOR EACH ANTLER)

Rnd 1: using Brown, sc 6 in a magic ring. (6 sts)

Rnd 2: [sc 2, inc] twice. (8 sts)

Rnds 3–8 (6 rnds): sc 1 in each st.

Do not fasten off. Cont joining tines.

Stuff firmly.

JOINING THE TINES

Rnd 9: still with long tine on hook, sc 1 in last st of small tine to join, PM here for new beg of rnd, sc 1 in each st of small tine, sc 1 in each st of long tine. (14 sts)

Rnd 10: [sc 5, dec] twice. (12 sts)

Rnd 11: [sc 1, dec] 4 times. (8 sts)

Rnd 12: sc 1 in each st.

Fasten off, leaving long tail for sewing.

Finish stuffing.

Sew antlers to top of cap over Rnds 11 and 12, 8 sts apart. Small tines should be facing inward.

Ears (make 2)

Rnd 1: using Brown, sc 6 in a magic ring. (6 sts)

Rnd 2: [sc 1, inc] 3 times. (9 sts)

Rnd 3: change to Light Brown, [sc 1, inc, sc 1] 3 times. (12 sts)

Rnd 4: sc 1 in each st.

Rnd 5: [sc 3, inc] 3 times. (15 sts)

Rnds 6–8 (3 rnds): sc 1 in each st.

Rnd 9: [sc 3, dec] 3 times. (12 sts)

Rnd 10: [sc 2, dec] 3 times. (9 sts)

Fasten off, leaving long tail for sewing.

Using Cream, embroider 3 straight stitches on each ear through same st at bottom to make ear tuft.

Do not stuff. Flatten ear, pinch sides of opening, and with yarn tail sew sides together to shape ear, using photo as a guide.

Sew ears on Rnds 11 and 12, 2 sts away from antlers.

Legs and body

LEG 1

Rnd 1: using Brown, sc 6 in a magic ring. (6 sts)

Rnd 2: inc in each st. (12 sts)

Rnd 3: [sc 5, inc] twice. (14 sts)

Rnds 4–5 (2 rnds): sc 1 in each st.

Rnds 6–14 (9 rnds): change to Light Brown, sc 1 in each st.

Fasten off. Set aside.

LEG 2

Work as for leg 1, but do not fasten off at end. Cont working on body.

IF NECESSARY, ADD A FEW MORE STITCHES ON LEG 2 TO ENSURE THE COLOR CHANGE IS AT THE BACK OF THE LEG.

BODY

Rnd 15: still with leg 2 on hook, ch 2, sc 1 in last st of leg 1 to join (see Techniques: Joining Legs), PM here for new beg of rnd, sc 1 in each st of leg 1, inc in each ch, sc 1 in each st of leg 2, inc in each ch. (36 sts)

Rnd 16: [sc 14, inc, sc 2, inc] twice. (40 sts)

Stuff legs firmly.

Rnds 17–20 (4 rnds): sc 1 in each st.

Rnd 21: change to White, slst 1 in each st loosely.

Rnd 22: work in BLO of Rnd 21 and both loops of Rnd 20 (see Techniques: Straight Stripe Color Change), sc 1 in each st. (40 sts)

Rnd 23: change to Pale Pink, sc 1 in each st.

Rnd 24: change to White, [sc 9, dec, sc 9] twice. (38 sts)

Rnd 25: change to Pale Pink, sc 1 in each st.

Rnd 26: change to White, [sc 17, dec] twice. (36 sts)

Rnd 27: change to Pale Pink, sc 1 in each st.

Rnd 28: change to White, [sc 5, dec, sc 5] 3 times. (33 sts)

Rnd 29: change to Pale Pink, sc 1 in each st.

Rnd 30: change to White, sc 1 in each st.

Rnd 31: change to Pale Pink, [sc 9, dec] 3 times. (30 sts)

Rnd 32: change to White, sc 1 in each st.

Rnd 33: change to Pale Pink, sc 1 in each st.

Rnd 34: change to White, [sc 3, dec] 6 times, turn. (24 sts)

Cont working in opposite direction.

Rnd 35: ch 2, work in BLO, dc 11, ch 3, slst 1, ch 3, dc 12, slst 1 to first st to join. (24 sts)

IF NECESSARY, ADJUST THE POSITION OF THE COLLAR SPLIT TO ALIGN WITH THE GAP BETWEEN THE LEGS.

Fasten off, leaving long tail for sewing.

Stuff body firmly.

SHIRT HEM DETAIL

Hold body with legs up and join White to first unworked loop of Rnd 22 with slst 1 (counts as first st of next rnd).

Rnd 1: slst 1 in each st. (40 sts)

Fasten off invisibly and weave in yarn ends.

Sew body to bottom of head using unworked loops from Rnd 34.

Arms (make 2)

Rnd 1: using Light Brown, sc 5 in a magic ring. (5 sts)

Rnd 2: inc in each st. (10 sts)

Rnds 3–5 (3 rnds): sc 1 in each st.

Rnd 6: change to White, slst 1 in each st loosely.

Rnd 7: work in BLO of Rnd 6 and both loops of Rnd 5, sc 1 in each st. (10 sts)

Rnd 8: change to Pale Pink, sc 1 in each st.

Rnd 9: change to White, sc 1 in each st.

Rnds 10–17 (8 rnds): rep Rnds 8 and 9 four more times.

Stuff lightly. Flatten opening and work next row through both layers to close (see Techniques: Closing with Single Crochet).

Row 18: sc 5. (5 sts)

Fasten off, leaving long tail for sewing.

SHIRT CUFF DETAIL

Hold arm with hand up and join White to first unworked loop of Rnd 6 with slst 1 (counts as first st of next rnd).

Rnd 1: slst 1 in each st. (10 sts)

Fasten off invisibly and weave in yarn ends.

Sew arms on each side of body between Rnds 33 and 34.

Tail

Rnd 1: using Light Brown, sc 6 in a magic ring. (6 sts)

Rnd 2: [sc 1, inc] 3 times. (9 sts)

Rnds 3–4 (2 rnds): sc 1 in each st.

Rnd 5: [sc 1, dec] 3 times. (6 sts)

Fasten off, leaving long tail for sewing.

Do not stuff. Sew tail to back of body on Rnd 18 (see Photo 4).

Pants

Start by making legs of pants.

PANT LEG 1

Using Dark Pink, ch 20, join to first ch with slst 1 to make a chain ring. Ch 1, start next rnd in same st.

Rnd 1: sc 1 in each ch working in back bump of ch. (20 sts)

Rnds 2–12 (11 rnds): sc 1 in each st.

Fasten off. Set aside.

PANT LEG 2

Work as for pant leg 1, but do not fasten off at end. Cont working on pants.

JOINING THE PANT LEGS

Rnd 13: still with pant leg 2 on hook, ch 1, sc 1 in first st of pant leg 1 to join, PM here for new beg of rnd, sc 1 in each st of pant leg 1, inc on ch, sc 1 in each st of pant leg 2, inc on ch. (44 sts)

Rnds 14–15 (2 rnds): sc 1 in each st.

IF NECESSARY, ADJUST THE POSITION OF THE CHAIN FOR THE HOLE FOR THE TAIL, MAKING SURE IT'S CENTERED AT THE BACK OF THE PANTS.

Rnd 16: sc 41, ch 3, skip next 3 sts. (44 sts)

Rnd 17: sc 41, sc 3 on ch. (44 sts)

Rnds 18–19 (2 rnds): sc 1 in each st.

Rnd 20: [sc 9, dec] 4 times. (40 sts)

Rnd 21: sc 9, end rnd here. (9 sts)

Fasten off invisibly and weave in yarn ends.

Fold first two rnds of each pant leg up.

Sew two small buttons to front of pants on Rnd 19, 10 sts apart (see Photo 5).

Straps

Row 1: using Dark Pink, ch 33, start in 7th ch from hook working in back bump of ch, slst 21, leave remaining ch unworked. (21 sts + 6 chs)

Row 2: ch 27, start in 7th ch from hook working in back bump of ch, slst 21, working in back bump of ch of remaining chs from Row 1, slst 6. (27 sts)

Fasten off, leaving long tail for sewing.

Sew bottom of Y-shaped straps to back of pants on Rnd 20.

Place pants on Dash the Deer, with tail through gap in base of pants, straps over arms, and secured at front on buttons.

4

5

6

Bow tie

Rnd 1: using Dark Pink, working in magic ring, [ch 2, dc 3, ch 2, slst 1] twice. (8 sts)

Fasten off, leaving long tail for shaping and sewing.

Wrap yarn tail 5 times around center of bow to shape it. Sew bow to front of body on Rnd 33.

Flower

Start by making blossom, leaf, and stem separately.

BLOSSOM

Rnd 1: using Pale Pink, ch 2, start in 2nd ch from hook, sc 6 in same st. (6 sts)

Cont working in a spiral.

Rnd 2: inc in each st. (12 sts)

Rnd 3: [sc 1, inc] 6 times. (18 sts)

Rnd 4: [sc 8, inc] twice. (20 sts)

Rnds 5–10 (6 rnds): sc 1 in each st.

Fasten off invisibly, leaving long tail for shaping.

Stuff firmly leaving last two rnds unstuffed. Pull yarn tail through 5th, 10th, 15th, and 20th sts and pull tightly to shape top of flower (see Photo 6). Weave in yarn end. Set aside.

LEAF

Rnd 1: using Yellow Green, ch 10, start in 2nd ch from hook working in back bump of ch, hdc 7, sc 1, slst 1, ch 1, cont working on other side of ch through both loops, slst 1, sc 1, hdc 6, [hdc 1, ch 1, slst 1] in same st. (19 sts)

Fasten off and weave in yarn ends. Set aside.

STEM

Rnd 1: using Yellow Green, sc 6 in a magic ring. (6 sts)

Rnds 2–5 (4 rnds): sc 1 in each st.

Leaf is attached in next rnd.

Rnd 6: sc 1 through bottom of leaf and next st of stem (see Photo 7), sc 5. (6 sts)

Rnds 7–15 (9 rnds): sc 1 in each st.

Fasten off, leaving long tail for sewing.

Stuff stem with piece of craft chenille stem, slightly longer than stem (see Photo 8). Insert leftover chenille stem through hole of Rnd 1 of blossom. Sew stem to bottom of blossom (see Photo 9).

7

8

9

Dawn

Head, muzzle, cap, and cheeks

Work as for Dash.

Ears

Work as for Dash.

Sew ears on Rnds 11 and 12 of cap, 16 sts apart at top.

Legs and body

LEG 1

Rnd 1: using Brown, sc 6 in a magic ring. (6 sts)

Rnd 2: inc in each st. (12 sts)

Rnd 3: [sc 5, inc] twice. (14 sts)

Rnds 4–5 (2 rnds): sc 1 in each st.

Rnds 6–14 (9 rnds): change to Light Brown, sc 1 in each st.

Fasten off. Set aside.

LEG 2

Work as for leg 1, but do not fasten off at end. Cont working on body.

IF NECESSARY, ADD A FEW MORE STITCHES ON LEG 2 TO ENSURE THE COLOR CHANGE IS AT THE BACK OF THE LEG.

BODY

Rnd 15: still with leg 2 on hook, ch 2, sc 1 in last st of leg 1 to join (see Techniques: Joining Legs), PM here for new beg of rnd, sc 1 in each st of leg 1, inc in each ch, sc 1 in each st of leg 2, inc in each ch. (36 sts)

Rnd 16: [sc 14, inc, sc 2, inc] twice. (40 sts)

Stuff legs firmly.

Rnds 17–20 (4 rnds): sc 1 in each st.

Rnd 21: change to Pale Pink, slst 1 in each st loosely.

Rnd 22: working in BLO of Rnd 21 and both loops of Rnd 20 (see Techniques: Straight Stripe Color Change), sc 1 in each st. (40 sts)

Rnd 23: sc 1 in each st.

Rnd 24: [sc 9, dec, sc 9] twice. (38 sts)

Rnd 25: sc 1 in each st.

Rnd 26: [sc 17, dec] twice. (36 sts)

Rnd 27: sc 1 in each st.

Rnd 28: [sc 5, dec, sc 5] 3 times. (33 sts)

Rnds 29–30 (2 rnds): sc 1 in each st.

Rnd 31: [sc 9, dec] 3 times. (30 sts)

Rnds 32–33 (2 rnds): sc 1 in each st.

Rnd 34: [sc 3, dec] 6 times, turn. (24 sts)

Cont working in opposite direction.

IF NECESSARY, ADJUST THE POSITION OF THE COLLAR SPLIT TO ALIGN WITH THE GAP BETWEEN THE LEGS.

Rnd 35: change to White, ch 2, work in BLO, dc 10, [dc 1, hdc 1, sc 1] in same st, slst 1, [sc 1, hdc 1, dc 1] in same st, dc 11, slst 1 to first st to join. (28 sts)

Fasten off, leaving long tail for sewing.

Stuff body firmly.

SHIRT HEM DETAIL

Hold body with legs up and join Pale Pink to first unworked loop of Rnd 22 with slst 1 (counts as first st of next rnd).

Rnd 1: slst 1 in each st. (40 sts)

Fasten off invisibly and weave in yarn ends.

Sew body to bottom of head using unworked loops from Rnd 34.

Arms (make 2)

Rnd 1: using Light Brown, sc 5 in a magic ring. (5 sts)

Rnd 2: inc in each st. (10 sts)

Rnds 3–12 (10 rnds): sc 1 in each st.

Rnd 13: change to Pale Pink, slst 1 in each st loosely.

Rnd 14: work in BLO of Rnd 13 and both loops of Rnd 12, inc in each st. (20 sts)

Rnd 15: sc 1 in each st.

Rnd 16: dec 10 times. (10 sts)

Rnd 17: sc 1 in each st.

Stuff lightly. Flatten opening and work next row through both layers to close (see Techniques: Closing with Single Crochet).

Row 18: sc 5. (5 sts)

Fasten off, leaving long tail for sewing.

SHIRT CUFF DETAIL

Hold arm with hand up and join White to first unworked loop of Rnd 13 with slst 1 (does not count as a st). Start next rnd in next st.

Rnd 1: [ch 2, slst 1] 10 times. (10 sts + 20 chs)

Fasten off invisibly and weave in yarn ends.

Sew arms on each side of body between Rnds 33 and 34.

Tail

Work as for Dash.

Skirt

Row 1: using Dark Pink, ch 9, start in 2nd ch from hook working in back bump of ch, sc 3, hdc 5, turn. (8 sts)

Row 2: work in BLO, ch 2, hdc 5, sc 3, turn. (8 sts)

Row 3: work in BLO, ch 1, sc 3, hdc 5, turn. (8 sts)

Row 4: work in BLO, ch 2, hdc 5, sc 3, turn. (8 sts)

Rows 5–40 (36 rows): rep Rows 3 and 4 eighteen more times.

Fasten off, leaving long tail for sewing.

Sew Row 40 to Row 1 to close skirt. Weave in yarn ends.

SKIRT WAISTBAND

Using Dark Pink, hold skirt up and join yarn to side of first row with slst 1 (does not count as a st). Start next rnd in same st.

Rnd 1: sc 1 in each side of rows. (40 sts)

Rnd 2: sc 1 in each st.

Fasten off invisibly and weave in yarn ends.

Place skirt on Dawn the Deer (see Photo 1).

Headband

Row 1: using Dark Pink, ch 91, start in 2nd ch from hook working in back bump of ch, slst 1, sc 1, hdc 1, dc 84, hdc 1, sc 1, slst 1. (90 sts)

Fasten off and weave in yarn ends.

Wrap headband around Dawn the Deer's head and tie a knot at top with ends (see Photo 2). Alternatively, sew headband on head.

MARCH

Harriet Hen & Gretel Goose

Harriet and Gretel may spend a lot of time running after goslings and chicks, but once a week they meet by the pond and chat about their favorite things. Gretel is a talented knitter who always shows up with some yarn and needles—and it looks like Harriet had to bring her youngest chick, Cooper, who couldn't stay put at home.

HARRIET 11.5CM (4½IN) GRETEL 13CM (5⅛IN)

DIFFICULTY LEVEL ☒☐☐

PATTERN NOTES

Most pieces are worked in a spiral without joining each round. The apron is worked in turned rows.

YOU WILL NEED

YARNS:

Hobbii Friends Cotton 8/4 (100% cotton) fingering (4-ply) weight, 160m (174yd) per 50g (1¾oz) ball, in the following shades:

FOR BOTH

- ✓ **White:** 1 ball in White (01)
- ✓ **Deep Pink:** 1 ball in Pink Berry Smoothie (54)
- ✓ **Blue:** 1 ball in Cornflower (83)

FOR HARRIET AND COOPER

- ✓ **Caramel:** 1 ball in Caramel (14)
- ✓ **Dark Yellow:** 1 ball in Dark Yellow (26)
- ✓ **Red:** 1 ball in Tomato (40)
- ✓ **Pale Blue:** 1 ball in Baby Blue (75)
- ✓ **Rust:** 1 ball in Cognac (17)
- ✓ **Bright Yellow:** 1 ball in Lemon Curd (22)

FOR GRETEL

- ✓ **Orange:** 1 ball in Peach (33)
- ✓ **Light Brown:** 1 ball in Nougat (09)

HOOK:

- ✓ 2.20mm (US B/1) crochet hook

TOOLS AND MATERIALS:

- ✓ 2 pairs of 6mm safety eyes
- ✓ 1 pair of 4mm safety eyes
- ✓ Yarn needle
- ✓ Toy stuffing
- ✓ Stitch markers
- ✓ Toothpicks or small knitting needles (optional)

Harriet

Head and body

Rnd 1: using Rust, sc 6 in a magic ring. (6 sts)

Rnd 2: inc in each st. (12 sts)

Rnd 3: [sc 1, inc] 6 times. (18 sts)

Rnd 4: [sc 2, inc] 6 times. (24 sts)

Rnd 5: [sc 3, inc] 6 times. (30 sts)

Rnd 6: [sc 4, inc] 6 times. (36 sts)

Rnd 7: [sc 5, inc] 6 times. (42 sts)

Rnd 8: sc 1 in each st.

Rnd 9: [sc 6, inc] 6 times. (48 sts)

Rnds 10–14 (5 rnds): sc 1 in each st.

Rnd 15: [sc 15, inc] 3 times. (51 sts)

Rnd 16: [sc 8, inc, sc 8] 3 times. (54 sts)

Rnds 17–18 (2 rnds): sc 1 in each st.

DO NOT CUT RUST, LEAVE YARN AT THE FRONT OF THE WORK (SEE PHOTO 1).

Rnd 19: change to Caramel, work in BLO, sc 1 in each st.

Rnd 20: [sc 17, inc] 3 times. (57 sts)

Rnd 21: [sc 9, inc, sc 9] 3 times. (60 sts)

Rnd 22: sc 1 in each st.

Rnd 23: [sc 19, inc] 3 times. (63 sts)

Rnd 24: [sc 10, inc, sc 10] 3 times. (66 sts)

Rnd 25: sc 1 in each st.

Rnd 26: inc, sc 1, inc, sc 7, inc, [sc 14, inc] 3 times, sc 7, [inc, sc 1] twice. (74 sts)

Rnd 27: sc 1 in each st.

Rnd 28: sc 17, inc, [sc 18, inc] twice, sc 17, inc. (78 sts)

Rnd 29: sc 1 in each st.

Rnd 30: sc 76, sc 1, [ch 4, start in 2nd ch from hook, sc 3 on ch, slst 1 at base of ch] 3 times (see Photo 2), sc 1. (78 sts + 3 tail feathers)

THE CH-4 AND SLST MAKE UP THE TAIL FEATHERS. THEY WILL BE SKIPPED IN THE NEXT ROUND.

Rnd 31: sc 77, go under tail feathers (see Photo 3), sc 1. (78 sts)

Place 6mm safety eyes between Rnds 12 and 13, 9 sts apart. Make sure tail feathers at back of body are centered with eyes.

Start stuffing, cont as you work.

Rnd 32: sc 1 in each st.

Rnd 33: [sc 11, dec] 6 times. (72 sts)

Rnd 34: sc 1 in each st.

Rnd 35: [sc 10, dec] 6 times. (66 sts)

Rnd 36: sc 1 in each st.

Rnd 37: [sc 9. dec] 6 times. (60 sts)

Rnd 38: [sc 8, dec] 6 times. (54 sts)

Rnd 39: [sc 7, dec] 6 times. (48 sts)

Rnd 40: [sc 6, dec] 6 times. (42 sts)

Rnd 41: [sc 5, dec] 6 times. (36 sts)

Rnd 42: [sc 4, dec] 6 times. (30 sts)

Rnd 43: [sc 3, dec] 6 times. (24 sts)

Rnd 44: [sc 2, dec] 6 times. (18 sts)

Rnd 45: dec 9 times. (9 sts)

Fasten off, sew hole closed by pulling yarn tail through front loops of remaining sts.

Using Deep Pink, embroider cheeks next to eyes in straight stitch (see Techniques: Straight Stitch). Make 2 horizontal lines for each cheek between Rnds 13 and 14, 2 sts wide.

Neck feathers

Go back to Rust on Rnd 18. Insert hook in unworked loop next to yarn and pull a loop (see Photo 4). Start next rnd in next st.

Rnd 1: sc 1 in each st. (54 sts)

ADD 1 ST TO ALIGN THE SCALLOPS WITH THE EYES.

Rnd 2: [skip 2 sts, dc 6 in same st, skip 2 sts, slst 1] 9 times. (9 scallops)

Fasten off and weave in yarn end.

Beak

Rnd 1: using Dark Yellow, sc 4 in a magic ring. (4 sts)

Rnd 2: sc 1, inc twice, sc 1. (6 sts)

Rnd 3: sc 2, inc twice, sc 2. (8 sts)

Fasten off, leaving long tail for sewing.

Stuff if necessary. Sew beak to the head centered with eyes between Rnds 12 and 14, with increases at top.

Wattle

Row 1: using Red, [ch 4, start in 2nd ch from hook, hdc 1, sc 1, slst 1] twice. (6 sts)

Fasten off, leaving long tail for sewing.

Sew wattle to head below beak.

Comb

Start by making individual bumps separately.

SMALL BUMP

Rnd 1: using Red, sc 6 in a magic ring. (6 sts)

Rnd 2: [sc 1, inc] 3 times. (9 sts)

Rnd 3: sc 1 in each st.

Fasten off. Set aside.

MEDIUM BUMP

Rnd 1: using Red, sc 6 in a magic ring. (6 sts)

Rnd 2: [sc 1, inc] 3 times. (9 sts)

Rnd 3: [sc 2, inc] 3 times. (12 sts)

Rnd 4: sc 1 in each st.

Fasten off. Set aside.

LARGE BUMP

Rnd 1: using Red, sc 6 in a magic ring. (6 sts)

Rnd 2: inc in each st. (12 sts)

Rnd 3: [sc 3, inc] 3 times. (15 sts)

Rnds 4–5 (2 rnds): sc 1 in each st.

Do not fasten off. Cont joining bumps to make comb.

JOINING THE BUMPS

Rnd 6: still with large bump on hook, sc 7 on large bump, sc 6 on medium bump, sc 9 on small bump, sc 6 on medium bump, sc 8 on large bump. (36 sts)

Rnd 7: sc 1 in each st.

Fasten off, leaving long tail for sewing.

Stuff bumps lightly. Use yarn tails to sew gaps between bumps.

Sew comb to top of head, aligned with beak, between Rnd 7 (at front) and Rnd 10 (on back, see Photo 5).

Left wing

Rnd 1: using Rust, sc 6 in a magic ring. (6 sts)

Rnd 2: inc in each st. (12 sts)

Rnd 3: [sc 1, inc] 6 times. (18 sts)

Rnd 4: [sc 2, inc] 6 times. (24 sts)

Rnd 5: [sc 3, inc] 6 times. (30 sts)

Rnd 6: [sc 4, inc] 6 times. (36 sts)

Rnd 7: [sc 5, inc] 6 times. (42 sts)

Do not stuff. Fold wing in half and work next row through both layers to close (see Techniques: Closing with Single Crochet).

Row 8: sc 11, [skip 1 st, hdc 5 in same st, skip 1 st, slst 1] twice, hdc 1, *dc 1, ch 3, slst 1* in same st. (26 sts)

Fasten off, leaving long tail for sewing.

Bring yarn tail to opposite corner of left wing.

Right wing

Work as for left wing for Rnds 1–7.

Do not stuff. Fold wing in half and work next row through both layers to close.

Row 8: ch 3, dc 1, hdc 1, [slst 1, skip 1 st, hdc 5 in same st, skip 1 st] twice, sc 11. (25 sts)

Fasten off, leaving long tail for sewing.

Sew wings on each corresponding side of body between Rnds 23 and 27, with "feathers" facing toward back and down. Sew only portion of wings between sewing pins as shown (see Photo 6).

Feet (make 2)

Start by making toes.

TOES (MAKE 2 FOR EACH FOOT)

Rnd 1: using Dark Yellow, sc 6 in a magic ring. (6 sts)

Rnds 2–3 (2 rnds): sc 1 in each st.

Fasten off first toe. Do not fasten off 2nd toe.

Do not stuff.

JOINING THE TOES

Rnd 4: still with 2nd toe on hook, sc 1 in last st of first toe to join, PM here for new beg of rnd, sc 1 in each st of first toe, sc 1 in each st of 2nd toe. (12 sts)

Rnd 5: [sc 2, dec] 3 times. (9 sts)

Rnd 6: [sc 1, dec] 3 times. (6 sts)

Rnd 7: sc 1 in each st.

Fasten off, leaving long tail for sewing, sew hole closed by pulling yarn tail through front loops of remaining sts.

Sew feet to front of body between Rnds 36 and 37, 6 sts apart (see Photo 7). Harriet the Hen should be able to sit on a surface.

Apron

The apron is worked in rows. Start each row with ch 2 (counts as first hdc).

Using Pale Blue, ch 20, and cont alternating Blue and White as given to make gingham pattern.

Row 1 (RS): start in 4th ch from hook working in back bump of ch, (Pale Blue) hdc 1, [(Blue) hdc 2, (Pale Blue) hdc 2] 4 times, turn. (18 sts)

Row 2: (White) ch 2, hdc 1, [(Pale Blue) hdc 2, (White) hdc 2] 4 times, turn. (18 sts)

Row 3: (Pale Blue) ch 2, hdc 1, [(Blue) hdc 2, (Pale Blue) hdc 2] 4 times. (18 sts)

Cont working around apron.

Rnd 4: change to White, ch 1, working on side of rows, [sc 1, ch 2] 4 times, working on foundation ch, [sc 1, ch 2] 18 times, working on side of rows, [sc 1, ch 2] 3 times, sc 1, ch, working on row 3, sc 18. (44 sts)

REMEMBER TO CARRY THE YARN ON THE WRONG SIDE OF THE FABRIC.

Fasten off invisibly and weave in yarn ends (see Techniques: Invisible Fasten Off).

Using White, cut 1 strand of 50cm (19½in) for apron strap. Run yarn ends through top corners of apron making a loop (see Photo 8). Place apron around Harriet the Hen's body with loop below wings. Make a bow with ends to secure. Tie a knot on both ends of strand to avoid splitting, trim excess yarn.

Cooper

Body

Rnd 1: using Bright Yellow, sc 6 in a magic ring (6 sts)

Rnd 2: inc in each st. (12 sts)

Rnd 3: [sc 1, inc] 6 times. (18 sts)

Rnd 4: [sc 2, inc] 6 times. (24 sts)

Rnd 5: sc 1 in each st.

Rnd 6: [sc 7, inc] 3 times. (27 sts)

Rnd 7: sc 1 in each st.

Rnd 8: [sc 8, inc] 3 times. (30 sts)

Rnd 9: sc 1 in each st.

Rnd 10: change to White, [sc 9, inc] 3 times. (33 sts)

Rnd 11: change to Blue, sc 1 in each st.

Rnd 12: change to White, sc 1 in each st.

Rnds 13-14 (2 rnds): rep Rnds 11 and 12 one more time.

Rnd 15: change to Yellow, sc 1 in each st.

Place 4mm safety eyes between Rnds 7 and 8, 6 sts apart.

Start stuffing, cont as you work.

Rnd 16: [sc 9, dec] 3 times. (30 sts)

Rnd 17: [sc 3, dec] 6 times. (24 sts)

Rnd 18: [sc 2, dec] 6 times. (18 sts)

Rnd 19: dec 9 times. (9 sts)

Fasten off, sew hole closed by pulling yarn tail through front loops of remaining sts.

Using Dark Yellow, embroider beak between eyes in straight stitch (see Techniques: Straight Stitch). Make 2 horizontal lines between Rnds 7 and 8, 2 sts wide.

Wings (make 2)

Row 1: using Bright Yellow, sc 5 in a magic ring, turn (5 sts)

Row 2: ch 1, inc in each st. (10 sts)

Cont working on side of rows.

Row 3: ch 1, sc 3. (3 sts)

Fasten off invisibly, leaving long tail for sewing.

Sew wings on each side of body between Rnds 11 and 13.

Feet

Row 1: using Dark Yellow, [ch 2, start in 2nd ch from hook, slst 1] 3 times, slst 1 in very first ch to shape foot. (3 toes)

Fasten off, leaving long tail for sewing.

Sew feet to front of body on Rnd 16, 4 sts apart.

Gretel

Head and body

Rnd 1: using White, sc 6 in a magic ring. (6 sts)

Rnd 2: inc in each st. (12 sts)

Rnd 3: [sc 1, inc] 6 times. (18 sts)

Rnd 4: [sc 2, inc] 6 times. (24 sts)

Rnd 5: [sc 3, inc] 6 times. (30 sts)

Rnd 6: [sc 4, inc] 6 times. (36 sts)

Rnd 7: [sc 11, inc] 3 times. (39 sts)

Rnd 8: [sc 6, inc, sc 6] 3 times. (42 sts)

Rnds 9–16 (8 rnds): sc 1 in each st.

Place 6mm safety eyes between Rnds 13 and 14, 9 sts apart. First eye should be between 15th and 16th sts, and 2nd between 24th and 25th sts.

Start stuffing, cont as you work.

Rnd 17: [sc 5, dec] 6 times. (36 sts)

Rnd 18: sc 7, [dec, sc 2] 6 times, sc 5. (30 sts)

Rnd 19: [sc 3, dec] 6 times. (24 sts)

Rnd 20: sc 3, [dec, sc 1] 6 times, sc 3. (18 sts)

Rnds 21–30 (10 rnds): sc 1 in each st.

Stuff neck firmly, cont stuffing body as you work.

Rnd 31: [sc 2, inc] 6 times. (24 sts)

Rnd 32: [sc 3, inc] 6 times. (30 sts)

Rnd 33: [sc 4, inc] 6 times. (36 sts)

Rnd 34: sc 1 in each st.

Rnd 35: [sc 5, inc] 6 times. (42 sts)

Rnd 36: sc 1 in each st.

Rnd 37: [sc 6, inc] 6 times. (48 sts)

Rnd 38: sc 1 in each st.

ADD OR UNDO A FEW STITCHES TO REACH THE STITCH IN THE MIDDLE OF THE BACK, CENTERED WITH THE EYES AT THE FRONT. THE FIRST STITCH OF THE NEXT ROUND WILL BE THE NEW BEGINNING OF THE ROUND.

Rnd 39: inc, sc 1, inc, sc 41, [inc, sc 1] twice, (52 sts)

Rnd 40: sc 1 in each st.

Rnd 41: [sc 12, inc] 4 times, (56 sts)

Rnd 42: sc 1 in each st.

Rnd 43: inc, sc 1, inc, sc 49, [inc, sc 1] twice. (60 sts)

Rnd 44: sc 1 in each st.

Rnd 45: sc 58, sc 1, [ch 4, start in 2nd ch from hook, sc 3 on ch, slst 1 at base of ch] 3 times (see Photo 1), sc 1. (60 sts + 3 tail feathers)

THE CH-4 AND SLST MAKE UP THE TAIL FEATHERS. THEY WILL BE SKIPPED IN THE NEXT ROUND.

Rnd 46: sc 59, go under tail feathers (see Photo 2), sc 1. (60 sts)

Rnd 47: [sc 8, dec] 6 times. (54 sts)

Rnd 48: sc 1 in each st. (54 sts)

Rnd 49: [sc 7, dec] 6 times. (48 sts)

Rnd 50: [sc 6, dec] 6 times. (42 sts)

Rnd 51: [sc 5, dec] 6 times. (36 sts)

Rnd 52: [sc 4, dec] 6 times. (30 sts)

Rnd 53: [sc 3, dec] 6 times. (24 sts)

Rnd 54: [sc 2, dec] 6 times. (18 sts)

Rnd 55: dec 9 times. (9 sts)

Fasten off, sew hole closed by pulling yarn tail through front loops of remaining sts.

Using Deep Pink, embroider cheeks next to eyes in straight stitch (see Techniques: Straight Stitch). Make 2 horizontal lines for each cheek between Rnds 14 and 15, 2 sts wide.

Beak

Rnd 1: using Orange, sc 4 in a magic ring. (4 sts)

Rnd 2: sc 1, inc twice, sc 1. (6 sts)

Rnd 3: sc 1, inc, sc 2, inc, sc 1. (8 sts)

Rnd 4: sc 3, inc twice, sc 3. (10 sts)

Rnd 5: sc 3, inc, sc 2, inc, sc 3. (12 sts)

Rnd 6: sc 5, inc twice, sc 5. (14 sts)

Fasten off, leaving long tail for sewing.

Stuff firmly. Sew beak to teh head centered with eyes between Rnds 11 and 15, with increases at top (see Photo 3).

Left wing

Rnd 1: using White, sc 6 in a magic ring. (6 sts)

Rnd 2: inc in each st. (12 sts)

Rnd 3: [sc 1, inc] 6 times. (18 sts)

Rnd 4: [sc 2, inc] 6 times. (24 sts)

Rnd 5: [sc 3, inc] 6 times. (30 sts)

Rnd 6: [sc 4, inc] 6 times. (36 sts)

Do not stuff. Fold wing in half and work next row through both layers to close (see Techniques: Closing with Single Crochet).

Row 7: sc 10, [hdc 4 in same st, slst 1] 3 times, hdc 1, *dc 1, ch 3, slst 1* in same st. (28 sts)

Fasten off, leaving long tail for sewing.

Bring yarn tail to opposite corner of left wing (see Photo 4).

Right wing

Work as for left wing for Rnds 1–6.

Do not stuff. Fold wing in half and work next row through both layers to close.

Row 7: ch 3, dc 1, hdc 1, [slst 1, hdc 4 in same st] 3 times, sc 10. (27 sts)

Fasten off, leaving long tail for sewing.

Sew wings on each corresponding side of body between Rnds 36 and 40, with "feathers" facing toward back and down. Sew only portion of wings between sewing pins as shown (see Photo 5).

Legs (make 2)

LEAVE A LONG TAIL AT THE START OF THE MAGIC RING ON THE OUTSIDE FOR SEWING LATER.

Rnd 1: using Orange, sc 6 in a magic ring. (6 sts)

Rnds 2–7 (6 rnds): sc 1 in each st.

Rnd 8: sc 3, end rnd here, turn. (3 sts)

Cont working in rows (see Photo 6).

Row A: ch 1, skip 1 st, sc 2, turn. (2 sts)

Row B: ch 1, skip 1 st, sc 1. (1 st)

Cont working in rnds (see Photo 7).

Rnd 9: sc 1 between rows, sc 3 on Rnd 8, sc 1 between rows, sc 1 on Row B. (6 sts)

Rnd 10: [sc 1, inc] 3 times. (9 sts)

Rnd 11: sc 1 in each st.

Rnd 12: [sc 2, inc] 3 times. (12 sts)

Rnd 13: sc 1 in each st.

Do not stuff. Flatten opening and work next row through both layers to close.

ADD OR UNDO A FEW STITCHES TO REACH THE CORNER OF ROUND 13.

Row 14: hdc inc, slst 1, hdc 1, ch 1, hdc 1, slst 1, *hdc 1, ch 2, slst 1* in same st. (8 sts)

Fasten off and weave in yarn ends.

Sew top of legs to bottom of body on Rnd 52, 4 sts apart (see Photo 8). Gretel the Goose should be able to sit on a surface.

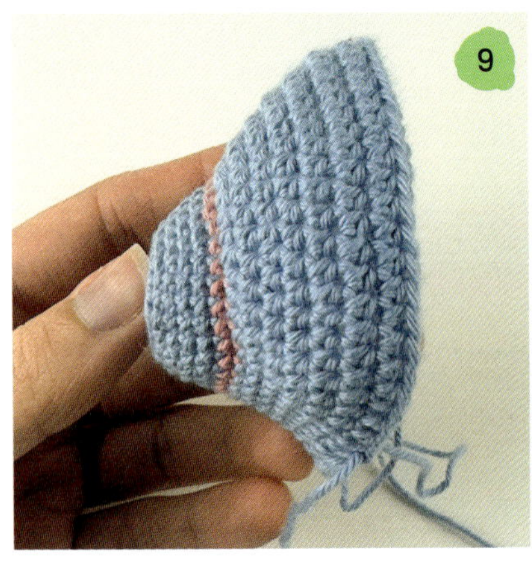

Hat

Rnd 1: using Blue, sc 8 in a magic ring. (8 sts)

Rnd 2: inc in each st. (16 sts)

Rnd 3: [sc 1, inc] 8 times. (24 sts)

Rnd 4: work in BLO, sc 1 in each st.

Rnd 5: [sc 3, inc] 6 times. (30 sts)

Rnd 6: sc 1 in each st.

Rnd 7: [sc 4, inc] 6 times. (36 sts)

Rnd 8: change to Deep Pink, sc 1 in each st.

Rnd 9: change to Blue, work in FLO, sc 6, [hdc 3, hdc inc] 6 times, sc 6. (42 sts)

Rnd 10: sc 6, hdc 30, sc 6. (42 sts)

Rnd 11: sc 6, [hdc inc, hdc 4] 6 times, sc 6. (48 sts)

Rnd 12: sc 6, hdc 36, sc 6. (48 sts)

Rnd 13: sc 6, [hdc 5, hdc inc] 6 times, sc 6. (54 sts)

Rnd 14: sc 6, hdc 42, sc 6. (54 sts)

Rnd 15: sc 3, hdc 48, sc 3. (54 sts)

Rnd 16: sc 3, end rnd here. (3 sts)

Fasten off invisibly and weave in yarn ends (see Techniques: Invisible Fasten Off).

Using Blue, cut 1 strand of 20cm (8in) for hat strap. Run yarn ends through 6th and 49th sts of Rnd 15 making a loop (see Photo 9). Place hat on Gretel the Goose's head with loop below head. Make a bow with ends to secure. Tie a knot on both ends of strand to avoid splitting. Trim excess yarn.

Shawl

The shawl is worked in rows starting with a magic ring. Starting chains from Rows 1–3 count as first dc and ch-1 sp (see chart).

Row 1: using Deep Pink, working in magic ring, ch 4, dc 3, ch 3, dc 3, ch 1, dc 1, tighten ring, turn. (8 sts)

Row 2: ch 4, dc 3 in ch-1 sp, ch 1, *dc 3, ch 3, dc 3* in ch-3 sp, ch 1, dc 3 in ch-1 sp, ch 1, dc 1 in 3rd ch of beginning ch-4 of Row 1, turn. (14 sts)

Row 3: ch 4, [dc 3 in ch-1 sp, ch 1] twice, *dc 3, ch 3, dc 3* in ch-3 sp, [ch 1, dc 3 in ch-1 sp] twice, ch 1, dc 1 in 3rd ch of beginning ch-4 of Row 2, turn. (20 sts)

Row 4: ch 1, dc 3 in ch-1 sp, slst 1 in 2nd dc st, [dc 6 in ch-1 sp, slst 1 in 2nd dc st] twice, dc 6 in ch-3 sp, slst 1 in 2nd dc st, [dc 6 in ch-1 sp, slst 1 in 2nd dc st] twice, dc 3 in ch-1 sp, slst 1 in 3rd ch of beg ch-4 of Row 3. (43 sts)

Fasten off and weave in yarn ends.

Using Deep Pink, cut 1 strand of 20cm (8in) for shawl strap. Run yarn ends through corners of shawl making a loop (see Photo 10). Place shawl on Gretel the Goose's back with loop at front. Make a bow with ends to secure. Tie a knot on both ends of strand to avoid splitting and trim excess yarn.

Chart for shawl

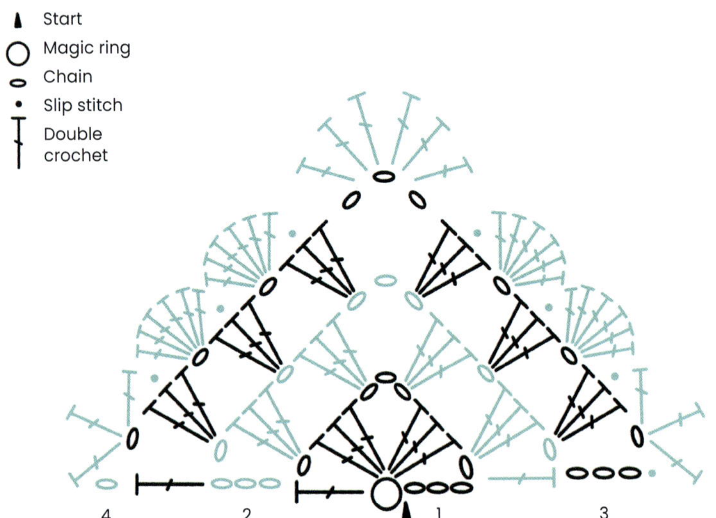

Basket

Rnd 1: using Light Brown, sc 7 in a magic ring. (7 sts)

Rnd 2: inc in each st. (14 sts)

Rnd 3: [sc 1, inc] 7 times. (21 sts)

Rnd 4: [sc 2, inc] 7 times. (28 sts)

Rnd 5: [sc 3, inc] 7 times. (35 sts)

Rnd 6: work in BLO, sc 1 in each st.

Rnd 7: [spike sc (see Techniques: Spike Single Crochet), sc 1 BLO] 17 times, spike sc. (35 sts)

Rnd 8: [sc 1 BLO, spike sc] 17 times, sc 1 BLO. (35 sts)

Rnds 9–10 (2 rnds): rep Rnds 7 and 8 one more time.

Rnd 11: slst 1 in each st loosely.

Cont making basket handle.

Row A: ch 21, slst 1 to opposite side of basket, slst 1 in next st of Rnd 11 (see Photo 11), turn. (21 chs + 2 sts)

Row B: ch 1, sc 21 around ch, slst 1 in st next to where ch started. (22 sts)

Fasten off and weave in yarn end.

Using Blue and Deep Pink, make small yarn balls to fill basket.

OPTIONAL: ADD TWO SMALL KNITTING NEEDLES OR TOOTHPICKS TO THE BASKET FOR A FINAL TOUCH.

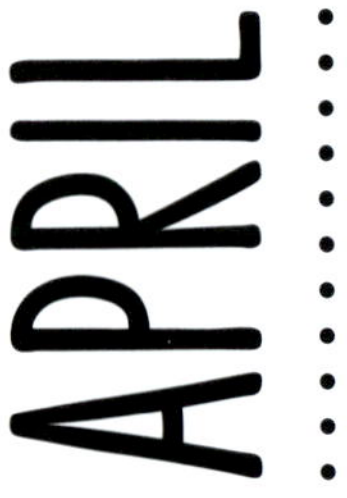

Leif Llama & Umee Unicorn

Everyone knows llamas and unicorns throw the best parties, and are the best guests. Leif the Llama came from South America to attend this anniversary celebration and even brought a special gift from his backyard. As for Umee the Unicorn, he brought a cupcake to blow out the candles. Are you ready to party with these two?!

LEIF
14.5CM (5¾IN)

UMEE
14CM (5½IN)

PATTERN NOTES

Most pieces are worked in a spiral without joining each round. The hair curls are worked in turned rows.

DIFFICULTY LEVEL

YOU WILL NEED

YARNS:

Hobbii Friends Cotton 8/4 (100% cotton) fingering (4-ply) weight, 160m (174yd) per 50g (1¾oz) ball, in the following shades:

FOR BOTH

- ✓ **White:** 1 ball in White (01)
- ✓ **Pink:** 1 ball in Candyfloss (45)
- ✓ **Light Brown:** 1 ball in Nougat (09)

FOR LEIF

- ✓ **Dark Yellow:** 1 ball in Dark Yellow (26)
- ✓ **Brown:** 1 ball in Cappuccino (10)
- ✓ **Yellow Green:** 1 ball in Pistachio (108)
- ✓ **Orange:** 1 ball in Peach (33)

FOR UMEE

- ✓ **Yellow:** 1 ball in Sunflower (24)
- ✓ **Mint:** 1 ball in Pastel Green (100)

HOOK:

- ✓ 2.20mm (US B/1) crochet hook

TOOLS AND MATERIALS:

- ✓ 2 pairs of 8mm safety eyes
- ✓ Stitch markers
- ✓ Yarn needle
- ✓ Toy stuffing
- ✓ Small pompom maker
- ✓ Cardboard
- ✓ Craft glue

Leif

Head

Rnd 1: using Dark Yellow, sc 6 in a magic ring. (6 sts)

Rnd 2: inc 6 times. (12 sts)

Rnd 3: [sc 1, inc] 6 times. (18 sts)

Rnd 4: [sc 2, inc] 6 times. (24 sts)

Rnd 5: [sc 3, inc] 6 times. (30 sts)

Rnd 6: [sc 4, inc] 6 times. (36 sts)

Rnd 7: [sc 5, inc] 6 times. (42 sts)

Rnd 8: [sc 6, inc] 6 times. (48 sts)

Rnds 9–11 (3 rnds): sc 1 in each st.

Rnd 12: [sc 7, inc] 6 times. (54 sts)

Rnds 13–18 (6 rnds): sc 1 in each st.

Rnd 19: [sc 7, dec] 6 times. (48 sts)

Rnd 20: [sc 6, dec] 6 times. (42 sts)

Rnd 21: [sc 5, dec] 6 times. (36 sts)

Place safety eyes between Rnds 14 and 15, 11 sts apart.

Start stuffing, cont as you work.

Rnd 22: [sc 4, dec] 6 times. (30 sts)

Rnd 23: [sc 3, dec] 6 times. (24 sts)

Rnd 24: [sc 2, dec] 6 times. (18 sts)

Rnd 25: [sc 1, dec] 6 times. (12 sts)

Rnd 26: dec 6 times. (6 sts)

Fasten off, sew hole closed by pulling yarn tail through front loops of remaining sts.

Muzzle

Rnd 1: using Light Brown, sc 6 in a magic ring. (6 sts)

Rnd 2: inc 6 times. (12 sts)

Rnd 3: [sc 1, inc] 6 times. (18 sts)

Rnd 4: [sc 2, inc] 6 times. (24 sts)

Rnds 5–7 (3 rnds): sc 1 in each st.

Fasten off, leaving long tail for sewing.

Using Brown, embroider nose on muzzle with straight stitch (see Techniques: Straight Stitch). Make a "V" from magic ring to Rnd 3, 4 sts apart at top, then add a vertical line below, 2 rnds tall, with curved smile at end between Rnds 2 and 3 (see Photo 1).

Sew muzzle to teh head centered with eyes, between Rnds 14 and 20 (see Photo 1). Stuff as you sew.

Cheeks (make 2)

Rnd 1: using Pink, sc 6 in a magic ring. (6 sts)

Rnd 2: inc 6 times. (12 sts)

Fasten off invisibly, leaving long tail for sewing (see Techniques: Invisible Fasten Off).

Sew cheeks next to eyes between Rnds 15 and 18 (see Photo 1).

Ears (make 2)

Rnd 1: using Dark Yellow, sc 6 in a magic ring. (6 sts)

Rnd 2: [sc 1, inc] 3 times. (9 sts)

Rnd 3: sc 1 in each st.

Rnd 4: [sc 2, inc] 3 times. (12 sts)

Rnds 5–9 (5 rnds): sc 1 in each st.

Rnd 10: [sc 2, dec] 3 times. (9 sts)

Fasten off, leaving long tail for sewing.

Using Light Brown, embroider 3 straight stitches on each ear through same st at bottom to make ear tuft (see Photo 1).

Do not stuff. Flatten ear, pinch sides of opening, and with yarn tail sew sides together to shape ear (see Photo 1).

Sew ears to top of head on Rnds 5 and 6.

Hair curls (make 3)

Row 1: using Dark Yellow, ch 22, start in 3rd ch from hook working in back bump of ch, hdc inc in each st. (40 sts)

Fasten off, leaving long tail for sewing.

Place hair curls between ears and sew on back of head between Rnds 4 and 5. Secure hair curls at front with a couple of sewn stitches (see Photos 1 and 2).

Front legs (make 2)

Rnd 1: using Brown, sc 6 in a magic ring. (6 sts)

Rnd 2: [sc 1, inc] 3 times. (9 sts)

Rnd 3: sc 1 in each st.

Rnds 4 and 5 (2 rnds): change to Light Brown, sc 1 in each st.

Rnd 6: change to Dark Yellow, working in FLO, [sc 2, inc] 3 times. (12 sts)

Rnds 7–12 (6 rnds): sc 1 in each st.

Fasten off, leaving long tail for sewing.

Stuff lightly.

Body

Rnd 1: using Dark Yellow, sc 6 in a magic ring. (6 sts)

Rnd 2: inc 6 times. (12 sts)

Rnd 3: [sc 1, inc] 6 times. (18 sts)

Rnd 4: [sc 2, inc] 6 times. (24 sts)

Rnd 5: [sc 3, inc] 6 times. (30 sts)

Rnd 6: [sc 4, inc] 6 times. (36 sts)

Rnd 7: [sc 5, inc] 6 times. (42 sts)

Rnd 8: [sc 6, inc] 6 times. (48 sts)

Rnds 9–13 (5 rnds): sc 1 in each st.

Rnd 14: [sc 14, dec] 3 times. (45 sts)

Rnds 15 and 16 (2 rnds): sc 1 in each st.

Rnd 17: [sc 13, dec] 3 times. (42 sts)

Front legs are attached in next rnd (see Techniques: Joining Front Legs).

Rnd 18: sc 15 on body, sc 7 on first front leg, skip 5 sts of body and of front leg, sc 1 on body, sc 7 on 2nd front leg, skip 5 sts of body and of front leg, sc 16 on body. (46 sts)

With yarn tail left on front legs sew unworked sts of front legs to skipped sts of body. Grab only loops on inside where body and front legs are joined. Secure middle of legs to body with a couple of sewn stitches.

Cont working around body and sts worked on front legs on Rnd 18.

Rnd 19: sc 1 in each st.

Rnd 20: sc 14, dec, sc 5, sc3tog, sc 5, dec, sc 15. (42 sts)

Rnd 21: [sc 6, dec, sc 6] 3 times. (39 sts)

Rnd 22: sc 1 in each st.

Rnd 23: [sc 11, dec] 3 times. (36 sts)

Rnd 24: [sc 4, dec] 6 times. (30 sts)

Rnd 25: [sc 3, dec] 6 times. (24 sts)

Stuff body firmly, cont as you work.

Rnd 26: sc 1 in each st.

Rnd 27: change to White, slst 1 in each st loosely.

Rnd 28: working in BLO of Rnd 27 and both loops of Rnd 26 (see Techniques: Straight Stripe Color Change), sc 1 in each st. (24 sts)

Change to Orange and then to Yellow Green to make collar.

Rnd 29: [(Orange) sc 3, (Yellow Green) sc 1] 6 times. (24 sts)

Rnd 30: [(Yellow Green) sc 1, (Orange) sc 1, (Yellow Green) sc 2] 6 times. (24 sts)

Rnd 31: change to White, sc 1 in each st.

Rnd 32: change to Dark Yellow, work in BLO, sc 1 in each st.

Rnd 33: sc 9, hdc 8, sc 2, slst 1, end rnd here. (20 sts)

Fasten off, leaving long tail for sewing.

Stuff neck firmly.

COLLAR DETAIL

Hold body upside down and join White to first unworked loop of Rnd 31 with slst 1 (counts as first st of next rnd) (see Techniques: Joining Yarn to Add a Detail).

Rnd 1: slst 1 in each st. (24 sts)

Fasten off invisibly and weave in yarn ends.

COLLAR RUFFLES

Hold body upside down and join Yellow Green to first unworked loop of Rnd 27 with slst 1 (does not count as a st). Start next rnd in same st.

Rnd 1: [sc 1, hdc 4 in next st, slst 1] 8 times. (48 sts)

Fasten off and weave in yarn end.

Sew body to bottom of head, with both front legs touching a flat surface and face facing forward, aligned with front legs.

Back legs (make 2)

Work as for front legs for Rnds 1–6.

Rnd 7 and 8 (2 rnds): sc 1 in each st.

Stuff firmly to here.

Rnd 9: sc 4, inc 4 times, sc 4. (16 sts)

Rnd 10: sc 6, inc 4 times, sc 6. (20 sts)

Rnds 11–14 (4 rnds): sc 1 in each st.

Stuff rest of back legs lightly.

Rnd 15: [sc 2, dec] 5 times. (15 sts)

Rnd 16: [sc 1, dec] 5 times. (10 sts)

Rnd 17: dec 5 times. (5 sts)

Fasten off, leaving long tail for sewing. Sew hole closed by pulling yarn tail through front loops of remaining sts.

Sew back legs on each side of body, between Rnds 8 and 13, slightly back from front legs. Leif the Llama should be able to sit on a flat surface.

Using Light Brown, make a small pompom for tail and attach it to back of body, between Rnds 7 and 8.

Rug

Rnd 1: using White, ch 8, start in 2nd ch from hook working in back bump of ch, inc, sc 5, sc 4 in last ch, turn, cont on other side of ch (see Techniques: Crocheting Around Foundation Chain) working through both loops, sc 5, inc in last ch. (18 sts)

Rnd 2: change to Orange, [inc twice, sc 5, inc twice] twice. (26 sts)

Rnd 3: change to Yellow Green, [sc 1, inc twice, sc 7, inc twice, sc 1] twice. (34 sts)

Rnd 4: change to White, [sc 3, [skip 1 st, dc 3 in next st, skip 1 st, slst 1] twice, skip 1 st, dc 3 in next st, skip 1 st, sc 3] twice. (34 sts)

Fasten off invisibly, leaving long tail for sewing.

Using Orange, cut 12 strands of 5cm (2in). Attach six strands on each side of rug to sc of Rnd 4 (see Techniques: Attaching Yarn Strands). Trim to desired length.

Sew rug to Leif the Llama's back between Rnds 14 and 22 (see Photo 3)

Cactus plant

Start by making pot and cactus separately.

POT

Rnd 1: using Orange, sc 5 in a magic ring. (5 sts)

Rnd 2: inc 5 times. (10 sts)

Rnd 3: [sc 1, inc] 5 times. (15 sts)

Rnd 4: working in BLO, sc 1 in each st.

Rnd 5: [sc 4, inc] 3 times. (18 sts)

Rnd 6: sc 1 in each st.

Cut a circle of cardboard to size of pot. Glue inside to keep bottom flat.

Rnd 7: [sc 5, inc] 3 times. (21 sts)

Rnd 8: sc 1 in each st.

DO NOT CUT ORANGE, LEAVE YARN AT THE FRONT OF THE WORK (SEE PHOTO 4).

Rnd 9: change to Brown, work in BLO, sc 1 in each st.

Rnd 10: [sc 5, dec] 3 times. (18 sts)

Stuff pot lightly.

Rnd 11: [sc 1, dec] 6 times. (12 sts)

Rnd 12: dec 6 times. (6 sts)

Fasten off, leaving long tail for sewing.

POT BRIM

Go back to Orange on Rnd 8. Insert hook in unworked loop next to yarn and pull up a loop. Start next rnd in next st (see Photo 5).

Rnds 1 and 2 (2 rnds): sc 1 in each st. (21 sts)

Rnd 3: work in FLO, hdc 1 in each st.

Fasten off invisibly and weave in yarn end.

Fold down Rnd 3.

CACTUS

Rnd 1: using Yellow Green, sc 5 in a magic ring. (5 sts)

Rnd 2: dc 2 in each st. (10 sts)

Rnds 3–7 (5 rnds): FPdc 1 in each st (see Techniques: Front Post Double Crochet).

Rnd 8: sc 1 in each st.

Fasten off, leaving long tail for sewing.

Stuff cactus and sew to top of pot (see Photo 6).

Umee

Head

Rnd 1: using White, sc 6 in a magic ring. (6 sts)

Rnd 2: inc 6 times. (12 sts)

Rnd 3: [sc 1, inc] 6 times. (18 sts)

Rnd 4: [sc 2, inc] 6 times. (24 sts)

Rnd 5: [sc 3, inc] 6 times. (30 sts)

Rnd 6: [sc 4, inc] 6 times. (36 sts)

Rnd 7: [sc 5, inc] 6 times. (42 sts)

Rnd 8: [sc 6, inc] 6 times. (48 sts)

Rnd 9: [sc 15, inc] 3 times. (51 sts)

Rnds 10–12 (3 rnds): sc 1 in each st.

Rnd 13: [sc 16, inc] 3 times. (54 sts)

Rnds 14–21 (8 rnds): sc 1 in each st.

Rnd 22: [sc 7, dec] 6 times. (48 sts)

Rnd 23: [sc 6, dec] 6 times. (42 sts)

Rnd 24: [sc 5, dec] 6 times. (36 sts)

Place safety eyes between Rnds 15 and 16, 11 sts apart.

Start stuffing, cont as you work.

Rnd 25: [sc 4, dec] 6 times. (30 sts)

Rnd 26: [sc 3, dec] 6 times. (24 sts)

Rnd 27: [sc 2, dec] 6 times. (18 sts)

Rnd 28: [sc 1, dec] 6 times. (12 sts)

Rnd 29: dec 6 times. (6 sts)

Fasten off, sew hole closed by pulling yarn tail through front loops of remaining sts.

Muzzle

Rnd 1: using Pink, sc 6 in a magic ring. (6 sts)

Rnd 2: inc 6 times. (12 sts)

Rnd 3: [sc 1, inc] 6 times. (18 sts)

Rnd 4: [sc 2, inc] 6 times. (24 sts)

Rnd 5: [sc 7, inc] 3 times. (27 sts)

Rnds 6–8 (3 rnds): sc 1 in each st.

Fasten off, leaving long tail for sewing.

Using White, embroider nostrils on muzzle with straight stitch (see Techniques: Straight Stitch). Make 1 vertical line over Rnd 4 for each nostril, 6 sts apart. Make 1 diagonal line over Rnd 4 for mouth, 4 sts wide, and 1 perpendicular line at top (see Photo 1).

Sew muzzle to the head centered with eyes, between Rnds 15 and 23. Stuff as you sew.

Cheeks (make 2)

Rnd 1: using Pink, sc 6 in a magic ring. (6 sts)

Rnd 2: inc 6 times. (12 sts)

Fasten off invisibly, leaving long tail for sewing (see Techniques: Invisible Fasten Off).

Sew cheeks next to eyes between Rnds 16 and 19 (see Photo 1).

Ears (make 2)

Rnd 1: using White, sc 6 in a magic ring. (6 sts)

Rnd 2: [sc 1, inc] 3 times. (9 sts)

Rnd 3: sc 1 in each st.

Rnd 4: [sc 2, inc] 3 times. (12 sts)

Rnds 5–7 (3 rnds): sc 1 in each st.

Rnd 8: [sc 2, dec] 3 times. (9 sts)

Fasten off, leaving long tail for sewing.

Do not stuff. Flatten ear, pinch sides of opening, and with yarn tail sew sides together to shape ear (see Photo 2).

Sew ears to top of head over Rnds 6 and 7 (see Photo 1).

Horn

Rnd 1: using Yellow, sc 6 in a magic ring. (6 sts)

Rnd 2: [sc 1, inc] 3 times. (9 sts)

Rnds 3 and 4 (2 rnds): sc 1 in each st.

Rnd 5: [sc 2, inc] 3 times. (12 sts)

Rnds 6 and 7 (2 rnds): sc 1 in each st.

Rnd 8: [sc 3, inc] 3 times. (15 sts)

Rnds 9 and 10 (2 rnds): sc 1 in each st.

Fasten off, leaving long tail for sewing.

Stuff firmly. Sew horn centered with ears, between Rnds 3 and 7 (see Photo 1).

Front legs (make 2)

Rnd 1: using Pink, sc 6 in a magic ring. (6 sts)

Rnd 2: inc 6 times. (12 sts)

Rnd 3: [sc 3, inc] 3 times. (15 sts)

Rnds 4 and 5 (2 rnds): sc 1 in each st.

Rnds 6–13 (8 rnds): change to White, sc 1 in each st.

Fasten off, leaving long tail for sewing.

Stuff lightly.

Body

Rnd 1: using White, sc 6 in a magic ring. (6 sts)

Rnd 2: inc 6 times. (12 sts)

Rnd 3: [sc 1, inc] 6 times. (18 sts)

Rnd 4: [sc 2, inc] 6 times. (24 sts)

Rnd 5: [sc 3, inc] 6 times. (30 sts)

Rnd 6: [sc 4, inc] 6 times. (36 sts)

Rnd 7: [sc 5, inc] 6 times. (42 sts)

Rnd 8: [sc 6, inc] 6 times. (48 sts)

Rnd 9: [sc 15, inc] 3 times. (51 sts)

Rnds 10–13 (4 rnds): sc 1 in each st.

Rnd 14: [sc 15, dec] 3 times. (48 sts)

Rnds 15 and 16 (2 rnds): sc 1 in each st.

Rnd 17: [sc 14, dec] 3 times. (45 sts)

Rnd 18: sc 1 in each st.

Front legs are attached in next rnd (see Techniques: Joining Front Legs).

Rnd 19: sc 15 on body, sc 8 on first front leg, skip 7 sts of body and of front leg, sc 1 on body, sc 8 on 2nd front leg, skip 7 sts of body and of front leg, sc 15 on body. (47 sts)

With yarn tail left on front legs, sew unworked sts of front legs to skipped sts of body. Grab only loops on inside where body and front legs are joined. Secure middle of legs to body with a couple of sewn stitches.

Cont working around body and sts worked on front legs on Rnd 19.

Stuff body firmly, cont as you work.

Rnd 20: sc 1 in each st. (47 sts)

Rnd 21: sc 14, dec, sc 6, sc3tog, sc 6, dec, sc 12, dec. (42 sts)

Rnd 22: [sc 6, dec, sc 6] 3 times. (39 sts)

Rnd 23: sc 1 in each st.

Rnd 24: [sc 11, dec] 3 times. (36 sts)

Rnd 25: sc 1 in each st.

Rnd 26: [sc 5, dec, sc 5] 3 times. (33 sts)

Rnd 27: sc 1 in each st.

Rnd 28: sc 9, dec, sc 1, hdc 8, hdc dec, hdc 1, sc 8, dec. (30 sts)

Fasten off, leaving long tail for sewing.

Sew body to bottom of head, with both front legs touching a flat surface, and with face facing forward aligned with front legs.

1

2

Back legs (make 2)

Work as for front legs for Rnds 1–5.

Rnds 6–8 (3 rnds): change to White, sc 1 in each st.

Stuff firmly to here.

Rnd 9: sc 5, inc 5 times, sc 5. (20 sts)

Rnd 10: sc 8, inc 4 times, sc 8. (24 sts)

Rnds 11–14 (4 rnds): sc 1 in each st.

Stuff rest of back legs lightly.

Rnd 15: [sc 2, dec] 6 times. (18 sts)

Rnd 16: [sc 1, dec] 6 times. (12 sts)

Rnd 17: dec 6 times. (6 sts)

Fasten off, leaving long tail for sewing, sew hole closed by pulling yarn tail through front loops of remaining sts.

Sew back legs on each side of body, between Rnds 8 and 13, slightly back from front legs. Umee the Unicorn should be able to sit on a flat surface.

Short mane curls (make 2)

Row 1: using Mint, ch 22, start in 3rd ch from hook working in back bump of ch, hdc inc in each ch. (40 sts)

Fasten off, leaving long tail for sewing.

Place short mane curls between ears on each side of horn and sew to top of head between Rnds 1 and 2. Secure short mane curls in front with a couple of sewn stitches (see Photo 3).

Long mane curls (make 3)

Row 1: using Mint, ch 42, start in 3rd ch from hook working in back bump of ch, hdc inc in each ch. (80 sts)

Fasten off, leaving long tail for sewing.

Place long mane curls between ears and sew them to top of head where you sewed short mane curls. Secure long mane curls on back of head with a couple of sewn stitches (see Photo 4).

Tail curls (make 3)

Row 1: using Mint, ch 27, start in 3rd ch from hook working in back bump of ch, hdc inc in each ch. (50 sts)

Fasten off, leaving long tail for sewing.

Sew tail curls to back of body between Rnds 7 and 8 (see Photo 5).

Bow tie

Row 1: using Yellow, ch 6, start in 3rd ch from hook working in back bump of ch, hdc 4, turn. (4 sts)

Rows 2–13 (12 rows): ch 2, hdc 4, turn. (4 sts)

Row 14: ch 2, hdc 4. (4 sts)

Fasten off, leaving long tail for sewing and shaping.

Sew short edges of bow tie together to make a ring.

Flatten ring with sewn edges in center, and wrap yarn tail tightly around a few times to shape bow.

Sew bow tie to body just below head.

3

4

5

Cupcake

Start by making frosting, base, candle, flame separately.

FROSTING

Rnd 1: using Pink, sc 6 in a magic ring. (6 sts)

Rnd 2: inc 6 times. (12 sts)

Rnd 3: [sc 1, inc] 6 times. (18 sts)

Rnd 4: [sc 2, inc] 6 times. (24 sts)

Rnds 5–8 (4 rnds): sc 1 in each st.

Rnd 9: work in FLO, [sc 1, hdc 3 in same st, slst 1] 8 times. (40 sts)

Fasten off and weave in yarn ends.

Stuff firmly.

BASE

Rnd 1: using Light Brown, sc 6 in a magic ring. (6 sts)

Rnd 2: inc 6 times. (12 sts)

Rnd 3: [sc 1, inc] 6 times. (18 sts)

Rnd 4: work in BLO, sc 1 in each st.

Rnd 5: [sc 5, inc] 3 times. (21 sts)

Rnd 6: sc 1 in each st.

Rnd 7: [sc 6, inc] 3 times. (24 sts)

Rnd 8: sc 1 in each st.

Fasten off, leaving long tail for sewing.

Cut a circle of cardboard to fit base. Glue inside to keep bottom flat (see Photo 6). Stuff firmly.

Sew base to unworked loops of Rnd 8 of topping. Add more stuffing as you sew.

CANDLE

Rnd 1: using Mint, sc 6 in a magic ring. (6 sts)

Rnd 2: work in BLO, sc 1 in each st.

Rnds 3–6 (4 rnds): sc 1 in each st.

Fasten off, leaving long tail for sewing.

Sew candle to top of frosting.

FLAME

Rnd 1: using Yellow, working in magic ring, sc 1, hdc 1, dc 1, ch 2, dc 1, hdc 1, sc 1, slst 1. (7 sts)

Fasten off, leaving long tail for sewing.

Sew flame to top of candle.

Bao Panda & Ben Bear

May brings with it the beauty of spring with blooming flowers and warm afternoons; the perfect excuse for Bao the Panda Bear and Ben the Grizzly Bear to meet for a picnic. Even though Ben just woke from hibernation it looks like he ate too much and fell back to sleep. Hopefully, he'll have room for a delicious lemon tart once he wakes up, baked with love by Bao.

BAO
12CM ($4\frac{3}{4}$IN)

BEN
14CM ($5\frac{1}{2}$IN)

PATTERN NOTES

Most pieces are worked in a spiral without joining each round. The straps and whipped cream are worked in turned rows. Although mainly Easy, Bao has some colorwork for the eye patches.

DIFFICULTY LEVEL

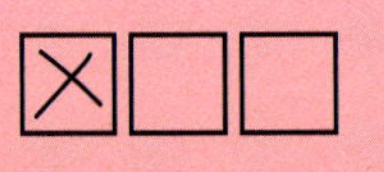

YOU WILL NEED

YARNS:

Hobbii Friends Cotton 8/4 (100% cotton) fingering (4-ply) weight, 160m (174yd) per 50g (1¾oz) ball, in the following shades:

FOR BOTH

- ✓ **White:** 1 ball in White (01)
- ✓ **Dark Gray:** 1 ball in Charcoal (123)
- ✓ **Deep Pink:** 1 ball in Pink Berry Smoothie (54)

FOR BAO

- ✓ **Teal:** 1 ball in Turkish Blue (88)
- ✓ **Yellow:** 1 ball in Sunflower (24)

FOR BEN

- ✓ **Light Brown:** 1 ball in Nougat (09)
- ✓ **Cream:** 1 ball in Oatmilk (03)
- ✓ **Brown:** 1 ball in Cappuccino (10)
- ✓ **Dark Pink:** 1 ball in Mulberry (55)
- ✓ **Bright Yellow:** 1 ball in Lemon Curd (22)

HOOK:

- ✓ 2.20mm (US B/1) crochet hook

TOOLS AND MATERIALS:

- ✓ 1 pair of 8mm safety eyes
- ✓ Stitch markers
- ✓ Yarn needle
- ✓ Toy stuffing
- ✓ Cardboard
- ✓ Craft glue

Bao

Head and body

Rnd 1: using White, sc 6 in a magic ring (6 sts)

Rnd 2: inc 6 times. (12 sts)

Rnd 3: [sc 1, inc] 6 times. (18 sts)

Rnd 4: [sc 2, inc] 6 times. (24 sts)

Rnd 5: [sc 3, inc] 6 times. (30 sts)

Rnd 6: [sc 4, inc] 6 times. (36 sts)

Rnd 7: [sc 5, inc] 6 times. (42 sts)

Rnd 8: [sc 6, inc] 6 times. (48 sts)

Rnd 9: [sc 15, inc] 3 times. (51 sts)

Rnd 10: [sc 8, inc, sc 8] 3 times. (54 sts)

Cont alternating from White to Dark Gray to make eye patches.

Rnd 11: (White) sc 19, (Dark Gray) sc 4, (White) sc 8, (Dark Gray) sc 4, (White) sc 19. (54 sts)

Rnd 12: (White) sc 18, (Dark Gray) sc 6, (White) sc 6, (Dark Gray) sc 6, (White) sc 18. (54 sts)

Rnds 13 and 14 (2 rnds): (White) sc 17, (Dark Gray) sc 7, (White) sc 6, (Dark Gray) sc 7, (White) sc 17. (54 sts)

Rnds 15 and 16 (2 rnds): (White) sc 16, (Dark Gray) sc 7, (White) sc 8, (Dark Gray) sc 7, (White) sc 16. (54 sts)

Rnd 17: (White) sc 17, (Dark Gray) sc 5, (White) sc 10, (Dark Gray) sc 5, (White) sc 17. (54 sts)

Cont working in White only.

Rnd 18: sc 1 in each st.

Place safety eyes between Rnds 14 and 15, on eye patches, 12 sts apart.

Rnd 19: [sc 17, inc] 3 times. (57 sts)

Rnds 20 and 21 (2 rnds): sc 1 in each st.

Rnd 22: [sc 9, inc, sc 9] 3 times. (60 sts)

Rnd 23: change to Dark Gray, sc 1 in each st.

Rnd 24: [sc 19, inc] 3 times. (63 sts)

Rnd 25: sc 1 in each st.

Rnd 26: [sc 10, inc, sc 10] 3 times. (66 sts)

Rnd 27: change to White, sc 1 in each st.

Rnd 28: [sc 21, inc] 3 times. (69 sts)

Rnd 29: [sc 11, inc, sc 11] 3 times. (72 sts)

Rnds 30–34 (5 rnds): sc 1 in each st.

Rnd 35: change to Teal, slst 1 in each st loosely.

Rnd 36: working in BLO of Rnd 35 and both loops of Rnd 34 (see Techniques: Straight Stripe Color Change), sc 1 in each st. (72 sts)

Rnds 37–41 (5 rnds): sc 1 in each st.

Start stuffing, cont as you work.

Rnd 42: [sc 10, dec] 6 times. (66 sts)

Rnd 43: [sc 9, dec] 6 times. (60 sts)

Rnd 44: [sc 8, dec] 6 times. (54 sts)

Rnd 45: [sc 7, dec] 6 times. (48 sts)

Rnd 46: [sc 6, dec] 6 times. (42 sts)

Rnd 47: [sc 5, dec] 6 times. (36 sts)

Rnd 48: [sc 4, dec] 6 times. (30 sts)

Stuff body firmly to this point to create a flat bottom.

Rnd 49: [sc 3, dec] 6 times. (24 sts)

Rnd 50: [sc 2, dec] 6 times. (18 sts)

Rnd 51: [sc 1, dec] 6 times. (12 sts)

Rnd 52: dec 6 times. (6 sts)

Fasten off, sew hole closed by pulling yarn tail through front loops of remaining sts.

Using Dark Gray, embroider eyebrows above eye patches in straight stitch (see Techniques: Straight Stitch). Make two diagonal lines on Rnd 9 for each eyebrow, 3 sts wide, using the photo as a guide.

SHORTS WAISTBAND DETAIL

Hold body up and join Yellow to first unworked loop of Rnd 35 with slst 1 (does not count as a st) (see Techniques: Joining Yarn to Add a Detail). Start next rnd in same st.

Rnd 1: sc 1 in each st. (72 sts)

Fasten off invisibly and weave in yarn ends (see Techniques: Invisible Fasten Off).

Using Yellow, embroider hearts around shorts. Make a double-V for each heart on Rnd 37, 2 sts wide, 4 sts apart (see Photo 1).

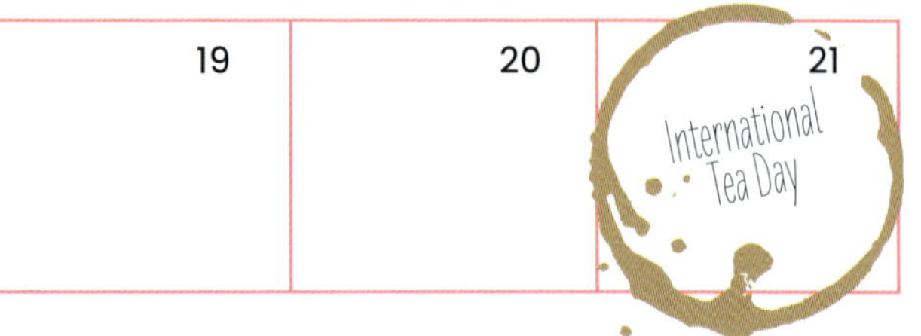

Muzzle

Rnd 1: using White, sc 6 in a magic ring. (6 sts)

Rnd 2: inc 6 times. (12 sts)

Rnd 3: sc 2, inc 3 times, sc 3, inc 3 times, sc 1. (18 sts)

Rnds 4 and 5 (2 rnds): sc 1 in each st.

Fasten off, leaving long tail for sewing.

Using Dark Gray, embroider nose on muzzle. Make 4 horizontal lines between Rnds 2 and 3, 5 sts wide. Add a vertical line centered with nose 3 rnds tall with a curved smile at bottom between Rnds 2 and 3.

Sew muzzle to the head between eyes, between Rnds 13 and 19. Stuff as you sew.

Cheeks (make 2)

Rnd 1: using Deep Pink, sc 6 in a magic ring. (6 sts)

Rnd 2: inc 6 times. (12 sts)

Fasten off invisibly and weave in yarn ends.

Sew cheeks next to eyes between Rnds 15 and 18.

Ears (make 2)

Rnd 1: using Dark Gray, sc 6 in a magic ring. (6 sts)

Rnd 2: inc 6 times. (12 sts)

Rnd 3: [sc 1, inc] 6 times.(18 sts)

Rnds 4 and 5 (2 rnds): sc 1 in each st.

Fasten off, leaving long tail for sewing.

Do not stuff. Flatten ears into semi-circles.

Inner ears (make 2)

Rnd 1: using Deep Pink, sc 6 in a magic ring. (6 sts)

Fasten off invisibly and weave in yarn ends.

Sew inner ears to inside of ears.

Sew ears on each side of head, in a curved position, between Rnds 5 and 10.

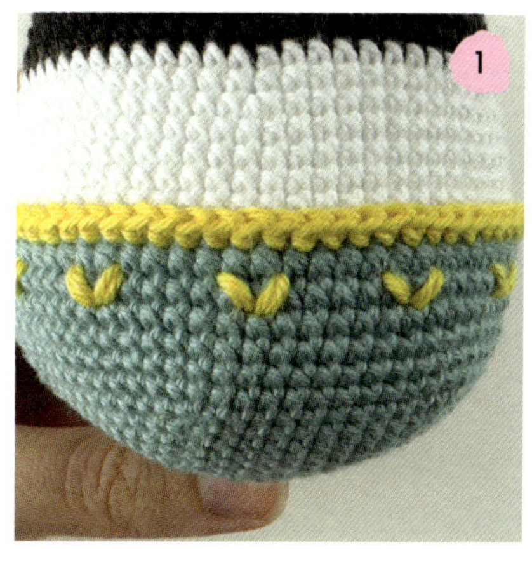

Legs (make 2)

Rnd 1: using Dark Gray, ch 7, start in 2nd ch from hook working in back bump of ch, hdc 4, hdc 2 in same ch, hdc 6 in last ch, turn, cont on other side of ch (see Techniques: Crocheting Around Foundation Chain) working though both loops, hdc 2 in same ch, hdc 4. (18 sts)

Rnd 2: hdc 2 in same st, hdc 5, [hdc 2 in same st] 6 times, hdc 5, hdc 2 in same st. (26 sts)

Rnds 3 and 4 (2 rnds): sc 1 in each st.

Rnd 5: sc 7, dec 6 times, sc 7. (20 sts)

Rnd 6: sc 8, dec twice, sc 8. (18 sts)

Rnds 7 and 8 (2 rnds): sc 1 in each st.

Stuff leg firmly to here.

Rnd 9: change to Teal, slst 1 in each st loosely.

Rnd 10: working in BLO of Rnd 9 and both loops of Rnd 8, sc 1 in each st. (18 sts)

Rnds 11 and 12 (2 rnds): sc 1 in each st.

.....

IF NECESSARY, ADD OR UNDO A FEW STITCHES TO REACH THE BOTTOM OF THE LEG.

....

Do not stuff rest of leg. Flatten opening and work next row through both layers to close (see Techniques: Closing with Single Crochet).

Row 13: sc 9. (9 sts)

Fasten off, leaving long tail for sewing.

Using White, embroider claws on legs with straight stitch. Make three lines, 1 for each claw, over Rnds 2 and 3, 2 sts apart.

SHORTS HEM DETAIL

Hold leg pointing down and join Teal to first unworked loop of Rnd 9 with slst 1 (does not count as a st) (see Techniques: Joining Yarn to Add a Detail). Start next rnd in same st.

Rnd 1: sc 1 in each st. (18 sts)

Fasten off invisibly and weave in yarn ends.

Sew legs on each side of body between Rnds 37 and 45. Add a couple of sewn stitches to hold middle of leg to body. Bao the Panda should be able to sit on a flat surface.

Arms (make 2)

Rnd 1: using Dark Gray, sc 6 in a magic ring (6 sts)

Rnd 2: inc 6 times. (12 sts)

Rnds 3–15 (13 rnds): sc 1 in each st.

Stuff lightly. Flatten opening and work next row through both layers to close.

Row 16: sc 6. (6 sts)

Fasten off, leaving long tail for sewing.

Sew arms on each side of body between Rnds 23 and 24 (see Photo 2).

Tail

Rnd 1: using Dark Gray, sc 6 in a magic ring. (6 sts)

Rnd 2: [sc 1, inc] 3 times. (9 sts)

Rnd 3: sc 1 in each st.

Fasten off, leaving long tail for sewing.

Sew tail to back of body between Rnds 43 and 45.

Bow tie

Rnd 1: using Yellow, working in magic ring, ch 2, dc 3, ch 2, slst 1] twice. (8 sts)

Fasten off, leaving long tail for shaping and sewing.

Wrap yarn tail five times around center of bow to shape. Sew bow tie to front of body, on Rnd 24.

Straps

Row 1: using Yellow, ch 37, start in 2nd ch from hook working in back bump of ch, sc 30, end row here. (30 sts)

Row 2: ch 31, start in 2nd ch from hook working in back bump of ch, sc 30, working in back bump of ch of remaining ch from Row 1, sc 6. (36 sts)

Fasten off, leaving long tail for sewing.

Sew bottom of Y-shape straps to back of body on shorts waistband (see Photo 2). Sew other two ends to front of body on shorts waistband, 20 sts apart.

Using Teal, embroider a French knot (see Techniques: French Knot) on straps at front where they overlap waistband.

Ben

Head and body

Rnd 1: using Light Brown, sc 6 in a magic ring. (6 sts)

Rnd 2: inc 6 times. (12 sts)

Rnd 3: [sc 1, inc] 6 times. (18 sts)

Rnd 4: [sc 2, inc] 6 times. (24 sts)

Rnd 5: [sc 3, inc] 6 times. (30 sts)

Rnd 6: [sc 4, inc] 6 times. (36 sts)

Rnd 7: [sc 5, inc] 6 times. (42 sts)

Rnd 8: [sc 6, inc] 6 times. (48 sts)

Rnd 9: [sc 15, inc] 3 times. (51 sts)

Rnd 10: [sc 8, inc, sc 8] 3 times. (54 sts)

Rnds 11–18 (8 rnds): sc 1 in each st.

Rnd 19: sc 17, inc, sc 9, inc, sc 8, inc, sc 17. (57 sts)

Rnds 20 and 21 (2 rnds): sc 1 in each st.

Rnd 22: sc 18, inc, sc 9, inc, sc 9, inc, sc 18. (60 sts)

Rnd 23: change to Deep Pink, slst 1 in each st loosely.

Rnd 24: work in BLO of Rnd 23 and both loops of Rnd 22 (see Techniques: Straight Stripe Color Change), sc 1 in each st. (60 sts)

Rnd 25: change to Dark Pink, sc 19, inc, sc 10, inc, sc 9, inc, sc 19. (63 sts)

Rnd 26: change to Deep Pink, sc 1 in each st.

Rnd 27: change to White, sc 20, inc, sc 10, inc, sc 10, inc, sc 20. (66 sts)

Rnd 28: change to Deep Pink, sc 1 in each st.

Rnd 29: change to Dark Pink, sc 21, inc, sc 11, inc, sc 10, inc, sc 21. (69 sts)

Rnd 30: change to Deep Pink, sc 22, inc, sc 11, inc, sc 11, inc, sc 22. (72 sts)

Rnd 31: change to White, sc 1 in each st.

Rnd 32: change to Deep Pink, sc 1 in each st.

Rnd 33: change to Dark Pink, sc 1 in each st.

Rnd 34: change to Deep Pink, sc 1 in each st.

Rnds 35–38 (4 rnds): As Rnds 31–34.

Rnd 39: change to Light Brown, work in BLO, sc 1 in each st.

Rnds 40 and 41 (2 rnds): sc 1 in each st.

Start stuffing, cont as you work.

Rnd 42: [sc 10, dec] 6 times. (66 sts)

Rnd 43: [sc 9, dec] 6 times. (60 sts)

Rnd 44: [sc 8, dec] 6 times. (54 sts)

Rnd 45: [sc 7, dec] 6 times. (48 sts)

Rnd 46: [sc 6, dec] 6 times. (42 sts)

Rnd 47: [sc 5, dec] 6 times. (36 sts)

Rnd 48: [sc 4, dec] 6 times. (30 sts)

Rnd 49: [sc 3, dec] 6 times. (24 sts)

Rnd 50: [sc 2, dec] 6 times. (18 sts)

Rnd 51: [sc 1, dec] 6 times. (12 sts)

Rnd 52: dec 6 times. (6 sts)

Fasten off, sew hole closed by pulling yarn tail through front loops of remaining sts.

Using Dark Gray, embroider eyes on head with straight stitches (see Techniques: Straight Stitch). Make 3 lines on Rnd 14 to draw each eye, 10 sts apart. First eye should be on 19th to 21st sts and 2nd on 32nd to 34th sts.

Using Cream, embroider eyebrows over eyes. Make two diagonal lines on Rnd 9 for each eyebrow, 3 sts wide.

SHIRT COLLAR DETAIL

Hold body up and join Deep Pink to first unworked loop of Rnd 23 with slst 1 (counts as first st of next rnd) (see Techniques: Joining Yarn to Add a Detail).

Rnd 1: slst 1 in each st. (60 sts)

Fasten off invisibly and weave in yarn ends (see Techniques: Invisible Fasten Off).

SHIRT HEM DETAIL

Hold body upside down and join Deep Pink to first unworked loop of Rnd 38 with slst 1 (counts as first st of next rnd).

Rnd 1: slst 1 in each st. (72 sts)

Fasten off invisibly and weave in yarn ends.

Muzzle

Rnd 1: using Cream, sc 6 in a magic ring (6 sts)

Rnd 2: inc 6 times. (12 sts)

Rnd 3: sc 2, inc 3 times, sc 3, inc 3 times, sc 1. (18 sts)

Rnds 4 and 5 (2 rnds): sc 1 in each st.

Fasten off, leaving long tail for sewing.

Using Brown, embroider nose on muzzle with straight stitches. Make 4 horizontal lines between Rnds 2 and 3, 5 sts wide, then a vertical line centered with nose 3 rnds tall and a side smile between Rnds 3 and 4, 2 sts wide.

Stuff firmly. Sew muzzle to the head between eyes, between Rnds 13 and 19.

Cheeks (make 2)

Rnd 1: using Deep Pink, sc 6 in a magic ring. (6 sts)

Rnd 2: inc 6 times. (12 sts)

Fasten off invisibly and weave in yarn ends.

Sew cheeks next to eyes between Rnds 15 and 18.

Ears (make 2)

Rnd 1: using Light Brown, sc 6 in a magic ring. (6 sts)

Rnd 2: inc 6 times. (12 sts)

Rnd 3: [sc 1, inc] 6 times. (18 sts)

Rnds 4 and 5 (2 rnds): sc 1 in each st.

Fasten off, leaving long tail for sewing.

Do not stuff. Flatten ears into semi-circles.

Inner ears (make 2)

Rnd 1: using Cream, sc 6 in a magic ring. (6 sts)

Fasten off invisibly and weave in yarn ends.

Sew inner ears to inside of ears.

Sew ears on each side of head, in a curved position, between Rnds 5 and 10.

Legs (make 2)

Rnd 1: using Light Brown, ch 7, start in 2nd ch from hook working in back bump of ch, hdc 4, hdc 2 in same ch, hdc 6 in last ch, turn, cont on other side of ch (see Techniques: Crocheting Around Foundation Chain) working though both loops, hdc in same ch, hdc 4. (18 sts)

Rnd 2: hdc 2 in same st, hdc 5, [hdc 2 in same st] 6 times, hdc 5, hdc 2 in same st. (26 sts)

Rnds 3 and 4 (2 rnds): sc 1 in each st.

Rnd 5: sc 7, dec 6 times, sc 7. (20 sts)

Rnd 6: sc 8, dec twice, sc 8. (18 sts)

Rnds 7–11 (5 rnds): sc 1 in each st.

IF NECESSARY, ADD OR UNDO A FEW STITCHES TO REACH THE BOTTOM OF THE LEG.

Stuff leg firmly until Rnd 8. Do not stuff rest of leg. Flatten opening and work next row through both layers to close (see Techniques: Closing with Single Crochet).

Row 12: sc 9. (9 sts)

Fasten off, leaving long tail for sewing.

Using Brown, embroider claws on legs using straight stitch. Make 3 lines, 1 for each claw, over Rnds 2 and 3, 2 sts apart.

Sew legs on each side of body between Rnds 40 and 42 in a diagonal position, 33 sts apart at top. Add a couple of sewn stitches where middle of leg touches body to keep in place. Ben the Grizzly Bear should be able to lay on a flat surface.

Arms (make 2)

Rnd 1: using Light Brown, sc 6 in a magic ring. (6 sts)

Rnd 2: inc 6 times. (12 sts)

Rnds 3–10 (8 rnds): sc 1 in each st.

Rnd 11: change to Deep Pink, slst 1 in each st loosely.

Rnd 12: working in BLO of Rnd 11 and both loops of Rnd 10, sc 1 in each st. (12 sts)

Rnd 13: change to Deep Pink, sc 1 in each st.

Rnd 14: change to White, sc 1 in each st.

Rnd 15: change to Dark Pink, sc 1 in each st.

Rnd 16: change to Deep Pink, sc 1 in each st.

Stuff lightly. Flatten opening and work next row through both layers to close.

Row 17: sc 6. (6 sts)

Fasten off, leaving long tail for sewing.

SHIRT CUFF DETAIL

Hold arm with hand up and join Deep Pink to first unworked loop of Rnd 11 with slst 1 (counts as first st of next rnd).

Rnd 1: slst 1 in each st (12 sts)

Fasten off invisibly and weave in yarn ends.

Sew arms on each side of body over Rnds 25 and 26. Arms should touch flat surface.

Tail

Rnd 1: using Light Brown, sc 6 in a magic ring. (6 sts)

Rnd 2: [sc 1, inc] 3 times. (9 sts)

Rnd 3: sc 1 in each st.

Fasten off, leaving long tail for sewing.

Sew tail to back of body between Rnds 43 and 45.

Lemon tart

Start by making crust, filling, and whipped cream separately.

CRUST

Rnd 1: using Brown, sc 6 in a magic ring. (6 sts)

Rnd 2: inc 6 times. (12 sts)

Rnd 3: [sc 1, inc] 6 times. (18 sts)

Rnd 4: [sc 2, inc] 6 times. (24 sts)

Rnd 5: [sc 3, inc] 6 times. (30 sts)

Rnd 6: work in BLO, sc 1 in each st.

Rnd 7: sc 1 in each st.

Rnd 8: working in FLO, [slst 1, sc 3 in same st, slst 1] 10 times. (10 shells)

Fasten off and weave in yarn ends.

Cut a circle of cardboard to size of crust. Glue inside to keep bottom flat.

FILLING

Rnd 1: using Bright Yellow, sc 6 in a magic ring. (6 sts)

Rnd 2: inc 6 times. (12 sts)

Rnd 3: [sc 1, inc] 6 times. (18 sts)

Rnd 4: [sc 2, inc] 6 times. (24 sts)

Rnd 5: [sc 3, inc] 6 times. (30 sts)

Fasten off, leaving long tail for sewing.

Sew Rnd 5 of filling to unworked loops of Rnd 7 of crust. Stuff as you sew.

WHIPPED CREAM

Row 1: using White, ch 13, start in 2nd ch from hook working in back bump of ch, inc 1 twice. (24 sts)

Fasten off, leaving long tail for sewing.

Curl whipped cream to create swirl and add a few sewn stitches to secure. Sew whipped cream to top of filling.

JUNE

Ella Elephant & Sully Sloth

June is the perfect month to travel the world and discover its wonders, just like Ella the Elephant and Sully the Sloth. Sully backpacked through the Swiss Alps and found the perfect souvenir for Ella, a cute little cow like those he saw in the mountains. Ella traveled to beautiful Japan, collecting miniatures from the places she visited – she brought a Daruma doll for her friend Sully.

ELLA 14CM (5½IN) SULLY 14CM (5½IN)

PATTERN NOTES

Most pieces are worked in a spiral without joining each round. The ears and bow are worked in turned rows, and the beanie and parts of the suitcase and backpack in closed rounds.

DIFFICULTY LEVEL ☒☒☒

YOU WILL NEED

YARNS:

Hobbii Friends Cotton 8/4 (100% cotton) fingering (4-ply) weight, 160m (174yd) per 50g (1¾oz) ball, in the following shades:

FOR BOTH

- ✓ **Light Blue:** 1 ball in Icy Blue (76)
- ✓ **Pale Pink:** 1 ball in Rose (44)
- ✓ **White:** 1 ball in White (01)
- ✓ **Red:** 1 ball in Tomato (40)
- ✓ **Mustard:** 1 ball in Mustard (28)

FOR ELLA

- ✓ **Yellow Green:** 1 ball in Pistachio (108)

FOR SULLY

- ✓ **Brown:** 1 ball in Cappuccino (10)
- ✓ **Light Brown:** 1 ball in Nougat (09)
- ✓ **Cream:** 1 ball in Oatmilk (03)
- ✓ **Blue:** 1 ball in Cornflower (83)

HOOK:

- ✓ 2.20mm (US B/1) crochet hook

TOOLS AND MATERIALS:

- ✓ 1 pair of 8mm safety eyes
- ✓ 1 pair of 6mm safety eyes
- ✓ Stitch marker
- ✓ Yarn needle
- ✓ Toy stuffing
- ✓ Sewing needle and black and white embroidery floss (thread)
- ✓ 4 small black beads
- ✓ 1.5mm craft wire
- ✓ Craft glue
- ✓ 1 small button
- ✓ 1 small gold craft bell
- ✓ Small pompom maker

Ella

Head

Rnd 1: using Light Blue, sc 6 in a magic ring. (6 sts)

Rnd 2: inc 6 times. (12 sts)

Rnd 3: [sc 1, inc] 6 times. (18 sts)

Rnd 4: [sc 2, inc] 6 times. (24 sts)

Rnd 5: [sc 3, inc] 6 times. (30 sts)

Rnd 6: [sc 4, inc] 6 times. (36 sts)

Rnd 7: [sc 5, inc] 6 times. (42 sts)

Rnd 8: [sc 6, inc] 6 times. (48 sts)

Rnd 9: [sc 15, inc] 3 times. (51 sts)

Rnds 10–13 (4 rnds): sc 1 in each st.

Rnd 14: [sc 8, inc, sc 8] 3 times. (54 sts)

Rnds 15 and 16 (2 rnds): sc 1 in each st.

Rnd 17: sc 22, ch 8 and skip 8 sts (see Photo 1), sc 24. (54 sts)

Rnd 18: sc 22, sc 8 on the ch, sc 24. (54 sts)

Rnds 19 and 20 (2 rnds): sc 1 in each st.

Place 8mm safety eyes between Rnds 16 and 17, 12 sts apart. Eyes should be 2 sts away on each side of gap of Rnd 17 (see Photo 2).

Start stuffing, cont as you work.

Rnd 21: [sc 7, dec] 6 times. (48 sts)

Rnd 22: [sc 6, dec] 6 times. (42 sts)

Rnd 23: [sc 5, dec] 6 times. (36 sts)

Rnd 24: [sc 4, dec] 6 times. (30 sts)

Rnd 25: [sc 3, dec] 6 times. (24 sts)

Rnd 26: [sc 2, dec] 6 times. (18 sts)

Rnd 27: [sc 1, dec] 6 times. (12 sts)

Rnd 28: dec 6 times. (6 sts)

Fasten off, sew hole closed by pulling yarn tail through front loops of remaining sts.

TRUNK

Using Light Blue, attach yarn with slst 1 (does not count as a st) to first unworked st of Rnd 16 of head (see Techniques: Joining Yarn to Add a Detail). Start next rnd in same st (see Photo 2).

Rnd 1: sc 8 on Rnd 16, sc 1 on side of gap, sc 8 on ch, sc 1 on side of gap. (18 sts)

Rnds 2–4 (3 rnds): sc 1 in each st.

Rnd 5: [sc 7, dec] twice. (16 sts)

Rnd 6: sc 1 in each st.

Start stuffing, cont as you work.

Rnd 7: [sc 3, dec, sc 3] twice. (14 sts)

Rnd 8: sc 1 in each st.

Rnd 9: [sc 5, dec] twice. (12 sts)

Rnd 10: sc 1 in each st.

Rnd 11: [sc 2, dec, sc 2] twice. (10 sts)

Rnd 12: sc 1 in each st.

Rnd 13: [sc 3, dec] twice. (8 sts)

Rnd 14: sc 1 in each st.

Fasten off, sew hole closed by pulling yarn tail through back loops of remaining sts.

Cheeks (make 2)

Rnd 1: using Pale Pink, sc 6 in a magic ring. (6 sts)

Rnd 2: inc 6 times. (12 sts)

Fasten off invisibly, leaving long tail for sewing (see Techniques: Invisible Fasten Off).

Sew cheeks next to eyes between Rnds 17 and 20 (see Photo 3).

Left ear

Rnd 1: using Light Blue, sc 4 in a magic ring, tighten ring, turn. (4 sts)

Row 2: ch 1, inc 4 times, turn. (8 sts)

Row 3: ch 1, [sc 1, inc] twice, [inc, sc 1] twice, turn. (12 sts)

Row 4: ch 1, [sc 1, inc, sc 1] 4 times, turn. (16 sts)

Row 5: ch 1, [sc 2, inc, sc 1] twice, [sc 1, inc, sc 2] twice, turn. (20 sts)

Row 6: ch 1, [sc 2, inc, sc 2] 4 times, turn. (24 sts)

Row 7: ch 1, [sc 3, inc, sc 2] twice, [sc 2, inc, sc 3] twice, turn. (28 sts)

Row 8: ch 1, sc 14, hdc 14. (28 sts)

Cont working around ear.

Rnd 9: ch 1, sc 16 on side of rows, ch 1, sc 28 on Row 8. (44 sts)

Fasten off invisibly, leaving long tail for sewing.

Right ear

Work as for left ear from Rows 1–7.

Row 8: ch 2, hdc 14, sc 14. (28 sts)

Cont working around ear.

Rnd 9: ch 1, sc 16 on side of rows, ch 1, sc 28 on Row 8. (44 sts)

Fasten off invisibly, leaving long tail for sewing.

Sew ears on each corresponding side of head, in a curved position, between Rnds 8 and 18. Ears should be about 4 sts away from cheeks at bottom (see Photo 3).

Legs and body

LEG 1

Rnd 1: using Light Blue, sc 8 in a magic ring. (8 sts)

Rnd 2: inc 8 times. (16 sts)

Cont alternating from Light Blue to White to make toes.

Rnd 3: working in BLO, [(Light Blue) sc 1, (White) 3-hdc puff (see Techniques: Puff stitch)] 3 times, (Light Blue) sc 10. (16 sts)

Cont working in Light Blue only.

Rnd 4: sc 1 in each st.

Rnd 5: [sc 7, inc] twice. (18 sts)

Rnds 6–9 (4 rnds): sc 1 in each st.

Fasten off. Set aside.

LEG 2

Work as for leg 1, but do not fasten off at end. Cont working on body.

BODY

Rnd 10: still with leg 2 on hook, ch 2, sc 1 in 10th st of leg 1 to join (see Techniques: Joining Legs), PM here for new beg of rnd, sc 1 in each st of leg 1, inc in each ch, sc 1 in each st of leg 2, inc in each ch. (44 sts)

Rnds 11 and 12 (2 rnds): sc 1 in each st.

Stuff legs firmly.

Rnd 13: [sc 8, inc, sc 2] 4 times. (48 sts)

Rnds 14 and 15 (2 rnds): sc 1 in each st.

Rnd 16: change to White, slst 1 in each st loosely. (48 sts)

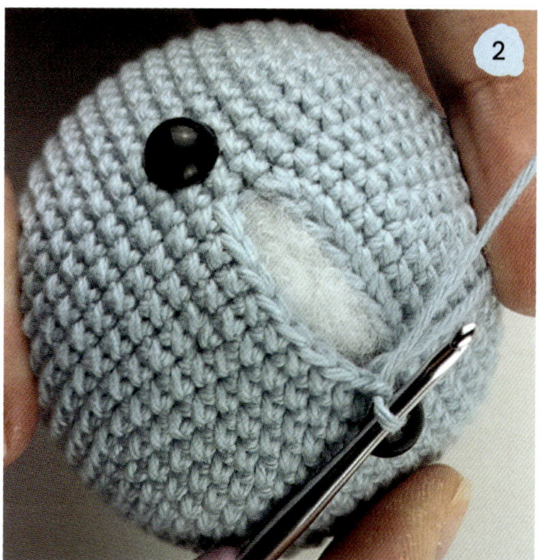

Rnd 17: working in BLO of Rnd 16 and both loops of Rnd 15 (see Techniques: Straight Stripe Color Change), sc 1 in each st. (48 sts)

Rnds 18 and 19 (2 rnds): sc 1 in each st.

Rnd 20: [sc 7, dec, sc 7] 3 times. (45 sts)

Rnd 21: sc 1 in each st.

Rnd 22: change to Yellow Green, sc 1 in each st.

Rnd 23: [sc 13, dec] 3 times. (42 sts)

Rnds 24 and 25 (2 rnds): sc 1 in each st.

Rnd 26: change to White, [sc 6, dec, sc 6] 3 times. (39 sts)

Rnd 27: sc 1 in each st.

Rnd 28: [sc 11, dec] 3 times. (36 sts)

Rnd 29: sc 1 in each st.

Rnd 30: change to Yellow Green, [sc 4, dec] 6 times. (30 sts)

Fasten off, leaving long tail for sewing.

Stuff body firmly.

SHIRT HEM DETAIL

Hold body with legs up and join White to first unworked loop of Rnd 16 with slst 1 (counts as first st of next rnd).

Rnd 1: slst 1 in each st. (48 sts)

Fasten off invisibly and weave in yarn ends.

Sew body to bottom of head.

Arms (make 2)

Rnd 1: using Light Blue, sc 6 in a magic ring. (6 sts)

Rnd 2: inc 6 times. (12 sts)

Rnds 3–9 (7 rnds): sc in each st.

Rnd 10: change to White, slst 1 in each st loosely.

Rnd 11: working in BLO of Rnd 10 and both loops of Rnd 9, sc 1 in each st. (12 sts)

Rnds 12–15 (4 rnds): change to Yellow Green, sc 1 in each st.

Rnd 16: change to White, sc 1 in each st.

Stuff lightly. Flatten opening and work next row through both layers to close (see Techniques: Closing with Single Crochet).

Row 17: sc 6. (6 sts)

Fasten off, leaving long tail for sewing.

SHIRT CUFF DETAIL

Hold arm with hand up and join White to first unworked loop of Rnd 10 with slst 1 (counts as first st of next rnd).

Rnd 1: slst 1 in each st. (12 sts)

Fasten off invisibly and weave in yarn ends.

Sew arms on each side of body between Rnds 29 and 30.

Tail

Row 1: using Light Blue, ch 7, start in 2nd ch from hook, slst 6. (6 sts)

Fasten off, leaving long tail for sewing.

Using Light Blue, cut 2 strands of 5cm (2in). Attach strands to tip of tail (see Techniques: Attaching Yarn Strands). Split strands for texture. Trim to desired length.

Sew tail to back of body on Rnd 14 (see Photo 4).

Bow

Start by making base, tie, and band separately.

BASE

Row 1: using Red, ch 36, start in 3rd ch from hook in back bump of ch, hdc 34, turn. (34 sts)

Rows 2–4 (3 rows): ch 2, hdc 34, turn. (34 sts)

Row 5: ch 2, hdc 34. (34 sts)

Fasten off, leaving long tail for sewing and shaping.

Sew short ends of base together to make a ring. Flatten ring with seam at center. Run yarn tail up and down through both layers across rows. Pull tightly to shape (see Photo 5).

TIE

Row 1: using Red, ch 12, start in 3rd ch from hook in back bump of ch, hdc 10. (10 sts)

Fasten off, leaving long tail for sewing.

Wrap tie around base piece where you shaped it. Sew short ends together on back. Weave in yarn ends.

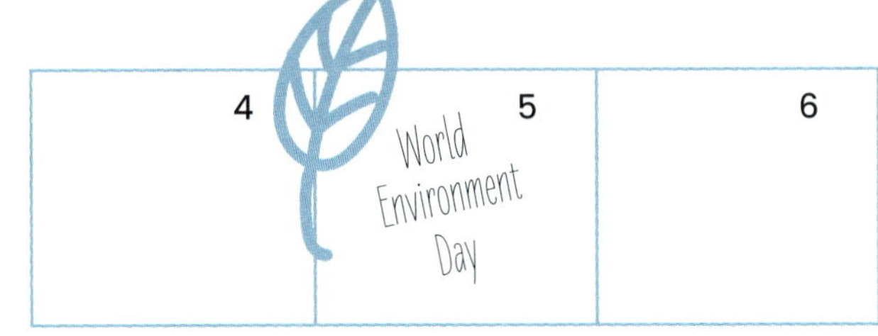

BAND

Using Red, ch 80.

Fasten off.

Run band through bottom of bow (see Photo 6). Place bow on top of head and tie a knot with ends of band on back of head. Alternatively, sew bow directly on head between ears.

Bunny bag

Rnd 1: using Pale Pink, ch 7, start in 2nd ch from hook working in back bump of ch, inc, sc 4, sc 4 in last ch, turn, cont on other side of ch (see Techniques: Crocheting Around Foundation Chain) working through both loops, sc 4, inc in last ch. (16 sts)

IF NECESSARY, ADJUST THE NUMBER OF CHAINS ON THE BAG STRAP TO FIT AROUND ELLA THE ELEPHANT.

Rnds 2–5 (4 rnds): sc 1 in each st.

Rnd 6: [sc 3, ch 4, start in 2nd ch from hook, slst 1, sc 2] twice, sc 10. (16 sts + 2 ears)

ADD OR UNDO A FEW STITCHES TO REACH THE STITCH BEFORE THE CORNER OF THE BUNNY BAG.

Rnd 7: slst 1, ch 42, slst 1 on opposite side of bag to join. (2 sts + 42 chs)

Fasten off and weave in yarn ends.

Embroider face details on bunny bag using straight stitch (see Techniques: Straight Stitch).

Using Light Blue, embroider eyes aligned with ears. Make 2 vertical lines on Rnd 4 for each eye, 3 sts apart.

Using Pale Pink, embroider cheeks next to eyes. Make 1 horizontal line between Rnds 3 and 4 for each cheek, each 1 st wide.

Using black embroidery floss, embroider nose between eyes. Make an "X" on Rnd 3.

Place bunny bag on Ella the Elephant as a crossbody bag.

4

5

6

Suitcase

Start by making base, outer layer, and inner layer separately.

BASES (MAKE 2)

Rnd 1: using Mustard, ch 8, start in 2nd ch from hook working in back bump of ch, sc 6, sc 3 in last ch, turn, cont on other side of ch working through both loops, sc 5, inc in last ch. (16 sts)

Rnd 2: [sc 3 in same st, sc 5, sc 3 in same st, sc 1] twice. (24 sts)

Rnd 3: [sc 1, sc 3 in same st, sc 7, sc 3 in same st, sc 2] twice. (32 sts)

Rnd 4: [sc 2, sc 3 in same st, sc 9, sc 3 in same st, sc 3] twice. (40 sts)

Rnd 5: [sc 3, sc 3 in same st, sc 11, sc 3 in same st, sc 4] twice. (48 sts)

Rnd 6: slst 1 in each st loosely.

Fasten off invisibly and weave in yarn ends.

OUTER LAYERS (MAKE 2)

Using Mustard, hold base upside down and join yarn to back loop of first st of Rnd 5 with slst 1 (does not count as a st). This part of outer layer is worked in closed rnds. Start each rnd with ch 1 and end with slst 1 on first st to join (see Photo 7).

Rnd 1: ch 1, working in BLO of Rnd 5, sc 1 in each st, slst 1 to first st to join. (48 sts)

Rnds 2–4 (3 rnds): ch 1, sc 1 in each st, slst 1 to first st to join.

Rnd 5: slst 1 in each st loosely.

Fasten off invisibly and weave in yarn ends.

Cut piece of wire approx. 10cm (4in) long. Bend in a "U" to make suitcase handle. Insert ends of wire through top of one outer layer and secure on inside with craft glue (see Photo 8).

Sew two small beads at bottom of each outer layer to make suitcase wheels (see Photo 8).

INNER LAYER 1

Rnd 1: using White, ch 8, start in 2nd ch from hook working in back bump of ch, sc 6, sc 3 in last ch, turn, cont on other side of ch working through both loops, sc 5, inc in last ch. (16 sts)

Rnd 2: [sc 3 in same st, sc 5, sc 3 in same st, sc 1] twice. (24 sts)

Rnd 3: [sc 1, sc 3 in same st, sc 7, sc 3 in same st, sc 2] twice. (32 sts)

Rnd 4: [sc 2, sc 3 in same st, sc 9, sc 3 in same st, sc 3] twice. (40 sts)

Begin working in closed rnds. Start each rnd with ch 1 and end with slst 1 on first st to join.

Rnd 5: ch 1, working in FLO, sc 1 in each st, slst 1 to first st to join. (40 sts)

Rnd 6: ch 1, sc 1 in each st, slst 1 to first st to join. (40 sts)

Fasten off invisibly and weave in yarn ends.

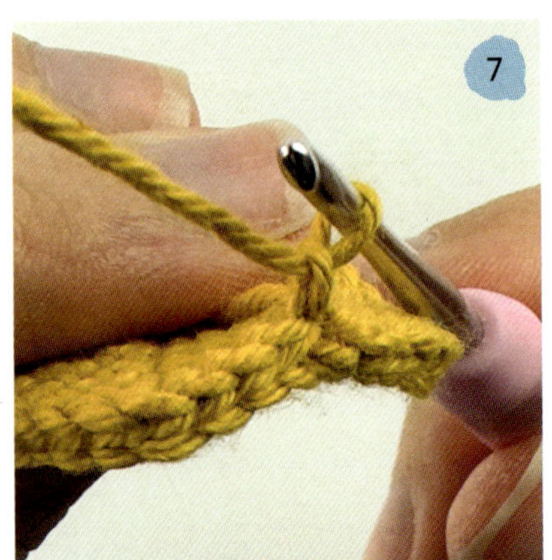

INNER LAYER 2

Work as inner layer 1 but do not fasten off at end. Cont working as follows.

Rnds 7–9 (3 rnds): ch 1, sc 1 in each st, slst 1 to first st to join. (40 sts)

Fasten off invisibly and weave in yarn ends.

Right side of fabric should be facing inward. Glue inner layers inside outer layers of suitcase. Tall inner layer should be inside outer layer with suitcase handle.

Using Mustard, cut a strand and sew one longer side of outer layers together. Use only back loops of Rnd 5 of outer layer, and join 13 sts together (see Photo 9).

Daruma doll souvenir

Rnd 1: using Red, sc 6 in a magic ring. (6 sts)

Rnd 2: inc 6 times. (12 sts)

Rnd 3: [sc 1, inc] 6 times. (18 sts)

Cont alternating from Red to White to make face patch.

Rnd 4: (Red) sc 7, (White) sc 4, (Red) sc 7. (18 sts)

Rnd 5: (Red) sc 6, (White) sc 6, (Red) sc 6. (18 sts)

Rnd 6: (Red) sc 3, inc, sc 2, (White) sc 6, (Red) sc 2, inc, sc 3. (20 sts)

Rnd 7: (Red) sc 8, (White) sc 4, (Red) sc 8. (20 sts)

Cont working in Red only.

Rnd 8: sc 1 in each st.

Rnd 9: sc 3, dec, sc 10, dec, sc 3. (18 sts)

Rnd 10: [sc 1, dec] 6 times. (12 sts)

Stuff firmly.

Rnd 11: dec 6 times. (6 sts)

Fasten off, sew hole closed by pulling yarn tail through front loops of remaining sts.

Embroider face details on face patch using straight stitch.

Using black embroidery floss, make 2 vertical lines for each eye on Rnd 6, on 2nd and 5th st. Make 1 horizontal line between eyes on Rnd 6, 1 st wide, for mouth. Make 1 diagonal line over eyes for each eyebrow.

Using Mustard, decorate Daruma doll with a few lines around face patch.

Place Daruma doll souvenir inside suitcase so Ella the Elephant can bring it home after her trip.

Sully

Eye patches (make 2)

Rnd 1: using Brown, ch 7, start in 3rd ch from hook working in back bump of ch, hdc 2 in same ch, hdc 3, hdc 4 in last ch, turn, cont on other side of ch (see Techniques: Crocheting Around Foundation Chain) working through both loops, hdc 3, hdc 2 in last ch. (14 sts)

Fasten off invisibly, leaving long tail for sewing (see Techniques: Invisible Fasten Off).

Head, body, and legs

Rnd 1: using Light Brown, sc 6 in a magic ring. (6 sts)

Rnd 2: inc 6 times. (12 sts)

Rnd 3: [sc 1, inc] 6 times. (18 sts)

Rnd 4: [sc 2, inc] 6 times. (24 sts)

Rnd 5: [sc 3, inc] 6 times. (30 sts)

Rnd 6: [sc 4, inc] 6 times. (36 sts)

Rnd 7: [sc 5, inc] 6 times. (42 sts)

Rnd 8: [sc 6, inc] 6 times. (48 sts)

Rnd 9: [sc 15, inc] 3 times. (51 sts)

Cont alternating from Light Brown to Cream to make face patch.

Rnd 10: (Light Brown) sc 18, (Cream) sc 12, (Light Brown) sc 21. (51 sts)

Rnd 11: (Light Brown) sc 17, (Cream) sc 14, (Light Brown) sc 20. (51 sts)

Rnds 12–17 (6 rnds): (Light Brown) sc 16, (Cream) sc 16, (Light Brown) sc 19. (51 sts)

Rnd 18: (Light Brown) sc 17, (Cream) sc 14, (Light Brown) sc 20. (51 sts)

Rnd 19: (Light Brown) sc 18, (Cream) sc 12, (Light Brown) sc 21. (51 sts)

Cont working in Light Brown only.

Rnd 20: [sc 16, inc] 3 times. (54 sts)

Rnd 21: sc 1 in each st.

Place 6mm safety eyes on eye patches on last ch before turning, then insert safety eyes on head between Rnds 14 and 15, 3 sts inside face patch on each side. Secure safety eyes inside head.

Sew eye patches to head in a tilted position, between Rnds 14 and 17, now or after stuffing.

Rnd 22: change to Blue, slst 1 in each st loosely. (54 sts)

Rnd 23: working in BLO of Rnd 22 and both loops of Rnd 21 (see Techniques: Straight Stripe Color Change), sc 1 in each st. (54 sts)

Rnd 24: sc 1 in each st.

Rnd 25: change to Light Blue, [sc 17, inc] 3 times. (57 sts)

Rnd 26: [sc 9, inc, sc 9] 3 times. (60 sts)

Rnd 27: sc 1 in each st.

Rnd 28: [sc 19, inc] 3 times. (63 sts)

Rnd 29: [sc 10, inc, sc 10] 3 times. (66 sts)

Rnds 30–34 (5 rnds): sc 1 in each st.

Rnd 35: change to Blue, sc 1 in each st.

Rnd 36: change to Light Brown, working in BLO, sc 1 in each st.

Rnd 37: [sc 9, dec] 6 times. (60 sts)

Rnd 38: [sc 4, dec, sc 4] 6 times. (54 sts)

Rnd 39: sc 1 in each st.

Stuff body firmly.

Divide body to make legs. Identify 8 sts at front and back of body for gap between legs, centered with eyes. PMs on first and last st on each side (see Photo 1). This leaves 19 sts for each leg. Cont working with leg 1.

ADD OR UNDO A FEW STITCHES TO REACH THE STITCH ON THE RIGHT OF THE FIRST MARKER ON THE BACK.

LEG 1

Rnd 40: still with body on hook, ch 5, sc 1 in first st on left of 2nd st marker at front of body to join, PM here for new beg of rnd, sc 18 on Rnd 39, sc 5 on ch (see Photos 2 and 3). (24 sts)

Rnd 41: [sc 3, dec, sc 3] 3 times. (21 sts)

Rnd 42: [sc 5, dec] 3 times. (18 sts)

Rnds 43 and 44 (2 rnds): sc 1 in each st.

Rnd 45: [sc 2, dec, sc 2] 3 times. (15 sts)

Rnd 46: [sc 3, dec] 3 times. (12 sts)

Rnd 47: [sc 1, dec] 4 times. (8 sts)

Stuff leg firmly.

Fasten off, sew hole closed by pulling yarn tail through front loops of remaining sts.

LEG 2

Join Light Brown with a slst 1 (does not count as a st) to first st on right of first st marker at front of body (see Techniques: Joining Yarn to Add a Detail).

Rnd 40: ch 5, sc 1 in first st on left of 2nd st marker at front of body to join, PM here for new beg of rnd, sc 18 on Rnd 39, sc 5 on ch. (24 sts)

Work as for leg 1 from Rnd 41 to end (see Photo 4).

FLAP

Using Light Brown, join yarn with slst 1 (does not count as a st) to first st with a marker at front of body. Remove st markers. Start next row in same st.

Rows 1–4 (4 rows): ch 1, sc 8, turn. (8 sts)

Row 5: ch 1, sc 8. (8 sts)

Fasten off, leaving long tail for sewing.

Finish stuffing body.

Sew Row 5 of flap to unworked sts at back of body. Then sew sides of flap to ch-5 of legs.

SWEATER TURTLENECK DETAIL

Hold body with legs up and join Blue to first unworked loop of Rnd 22 with slst 1 (counts as first st of next rnd).

Rnd 1: slst 1 in each st. (54 sts)

Fasten off invisibly and weave in yarn ends.

SWEATER HEM DETAIL

Hold body with legs up and join Blue to first unworked loop of Rnd 35 with slst 1 (counts as first st of next rnd).

Rnd 1: slst 1 in each st. (66 sts)

Fasten off invisibly and weave in yarn ends.

SWEATER EMBROIDERY

Using white embroidery floss, embroider a snowflake on middle section of sweater, centered with eyes. Use photos for reference. Then embroider a few French knots around snowflake (see Techniques: French Knot).

Nose

Rnd 1: using Brown, ch 4, start in 2nd ch from hook working in back bump of ch, sc 2, sc 3 in last ch, turn, cont on other side of ch working through both loops, sc 1, inc in last ch. (8 sts)

Fasten off invisibly, leaving long tail for sewing.

Sew nose between eyes over Rnds 14 and 15.

Embroider face details using straight stitch (see Techniques: Straight Stitch).

Using Brown, embroider mouth below nose. Make a "V" on Rnd 17, 3 sts wide.

Using Pale Pink, embroider cheeks below eye patches. Make three horizontal lines for each cheek between Rnds 17 and 18, 2 sts wide.

Arms (make 2)

Rnd 1: using Light Brown, sc 6 in a magic ring. (6 sts)

Rnd 2: inc 6 times. (12 sts)

Rnds 3–5 (3 rnds): sc 1 in each st.

Rnd 6: change to Blue, slst 1 in each st loosely.

Rnd 7: working in BLO of Rnd 6 and both loops of Rnd 5, sc 1 in each st. (12 sts)

Rnds 8–17 (10 rnds): change to Light Blue, sc 1 in each st.

Stuff lightly. Flatten opening and work next row through both layers to close (see Techniques: Closing with Single Crochet).

Row 18: sc 6. (6 sts)

Fasten off, leaving long tail for sewing.

SWEATER CUFF DETAIL

Hold arm with hand up and join Blue to first unworked loop of Rnd 6 with slst 1 (counts as first st of next rnd).

Rnd 1: slst 1 in each st. (12 sts)

Fasten off invisibly and weave in yarn ends.

Sew arms on each side of body between Rnds 25 and 26.

Claws (make 4)

Row 1: using Cream, [ch 4, starting in 2nd ch from hook, slst 3] 3 times. (3 fingers)

Fasten off, leaving long tail for sewing.

Sew one claw on each arm on Rnds 1 and 2 and one on each leg between Rnds 46 and 47.

Beanie

Worked in closed rnds starting with a magic ring. Start each rnd with ch 2 (counts as first half double crochet), and end with slst 1 on top of ch-2 (does not count as a st).

Rnd 1: using Red, ch 2, hdc 7 in a magic ring, slst 1 to ch-2 to join. (8 sts)

Rnd 2: ch 2, hdc 1 in same st as ch, hdc 2 in same st 7 times, slst 1 to ch-2 to join. (16 sts)

Rnd 3: ch 2, hdc 2 in same st, [hdc 1, hdc 2 in same st] 7 times, slst 1 to ch-2 to join. (24 sts)

Rnd 4: ch 2, hdc 1, hdc 2 in same st, [hdc 2, hdc 2 in same st] 7 times, slst 1 to ch-2 to join. (32 sts)

Rnd 5: ch 2, hdc 2, hdc 2 in same st, [hdc 3, hdc 2 in same st] 7 times, slst 1 to ch-2 to join. (40 sts)

Rnd 6: ch 2, hdc 3, hdc 2 in same st, [hdc 4, hdc 2 in same st] 7 times, slst 1 to ch-2 to join. (48 sts)

Rnds 7–12 (6 rnds): ch 2, hdc 47, slst 1 to ch-2 to join. (48 sts)

Fasten off and weave in yarn end.

Using White, make a small pompom and attach to top of beanie. Fold up Rnds 11 and 12 of beanie to create a brim. Place beanie on Sully the Sloth's head.

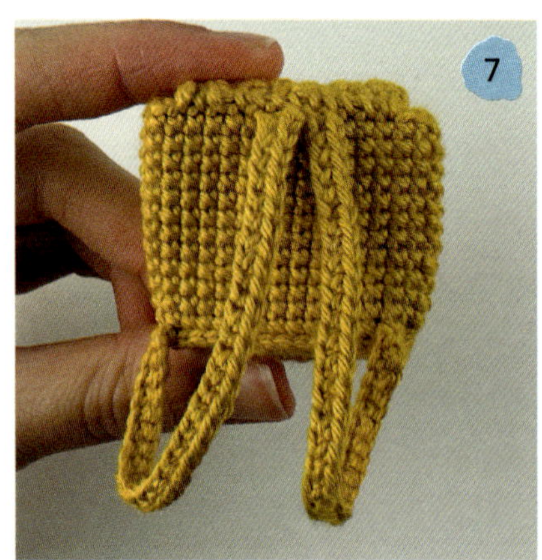

Backpack

Start by making base, body, flap, and straps separately.

BASE

Rnd 1: using Mustard, ch 11, start in 2nd ch from hook working in back bump of ch, inc, sc 8, sc 4 in last ch, turn, cont on other side of ch working through both loops, sc 8, inc in last ch. (24 sts)

Rnd 2: [inc twice, sc 8, inc twice] twice. (32 sts)

Rnd 3: slst 1 in each st loosely.

Fasten off invisibly and weave in yarn ends.

BODY

Hold base upside down and join Mustard to back loop of first st of Rnd 2 with slst 1 (does not count as a st). This part is worked in closed rnds. Start each rnd with ch 1, end with slst 1 on first st to join.

Rnd 1: ch 1, working in BLO of Rnd 2, sc 1 in each st, slst 1 to first st to join. (32 sts)

Rnds 2–12 (11 rnds): ch 1, sc 1 in each st, slst 1 to first st to join. (32 sts)

Fasten off invisibly and weave in yarn ends.

FLAP

Row 1: using Mustard, ch 6, start in 2nd ch from hook working in back bump of ch, sc 4, sc 4 in last ch, turn, cont on other side of ch working through both loops, sc 4, turn. (12 sts)

Row 2: ch 1, sc 4, inc 4 times, sc 4, turn. (16 sts)

Row 3: ch 1, sc 6, inc 4 times, sc 6, turn. (20 sts)

Row 4: ch 1, sc 8, inc 4 times, sc 8, turn. (24 sts)

Row 5: ch 1, sc 10, inc 4 times, sc 10, turn. (28 sts)

....

IF NECESSARY, ADJUST THE NUMBER OF BUTTONHOLE CHAINS TO FIT AROUND THE BUTTON.

....

Row 6: ch 1, sc 10, [inc, sc 1] twice, ch 6 to make buttonhole, [sc 1, inc] twice, sc 10. (32 sts + 6 chs)

Fasten off, leaving long tail for sewing.

Flatten opening of backpack body in same direction as foundation chain. Identify 12 sts on back and sew side of rows of backpack flap to sts (see Photo 5).

Sew a small button to front of backpack on Rnd 9. Close backpack by placing chain around button.

STRAPS (MAKE 2)

....

IF NECESSARY, ADJUST THE NUMBER OF STRAP CHAINS TO FIT AROUND THE ARMS OF SULLY THE SLOTH.

....

Row 1: using Mustard, ch 33, attach ch with slst 1 to st of Rnd 1 of body near corner (see Photo 6), ch 1, start in 2nd ch from hook working in back bump of ch, sc 33. (34 sts)

Fasten off, leaving long tail for sewing.

Sew other end of strap to middle back of backpack between Rnds 13 and 14.

For 2nd strap, attach chain 12 sts away from first strap at bottom, and next first strap at top (see Photo 7).

Place backpack on Sully the Sloth with straps around arms.

Cow souvenir

Start by making head and body, and snout separately.

HEAD AND BODY

Rnd 1: using Cream, sc 6 in a magic ring. (6 sts)

Rnd 2: inc 6 times. (12 sts)

Cont alternating from Cream to Brown to make the horns.

Rnd 3: (Cream) sc 1, inc, sc 1, *sc 1, (Brown) picot (see Techniques: Picot Stitch), (Cream) sc 1* in same st, [sc 1, inc] twice, sc 1, (Brown) picot, (Cream) inc, sc 1, inc. (18 sts)

Cont working in Cream only.

Rnd 4: sc 5, skip picot, inc, sc 5, inc, sc 1, skip picot, sc 4, inc. (21 sts + 2 horns)

Rnd 5: sc 5, *dc 1, ch 2, dc 1, slst 1* in same st, sc 9, *dc 1, ch 2, dc 1, slst 1* in same st, sc 5. (25 sts + 4 chs)

Rnd 6: sc 5, skip *dc 1, ch 2, dc 1*, sc 10, skip *dc 1, ch 2, dc 1*, sc 6. (21 sts)

Rnds 7 and 8 (2 rnds): sc 1 in each st.

Rnd 9: dec 5 times, sc 1, dec 4 times, sc 2. (12 sts)

Stuff head firmly.

Rnd 10: slst 1 in each st loosely.

Rnd 11: [sc 3, inc] 3 times. (15 sts)

Cont alternating from Cream to Red to make patches.

Rnd 12: (Cream) sc 4, 4-dc bobble (see Techniques: Bobble Stitch), sc 1, (Red) sc 1, (Cream) sc 2, 4-dc bobble, sc 2, (Red) sc 2, (Cream) sc 1. (15 sts)

Rnd 13: (Cream) sc 6, (Red) sc 2, (Cream) sc 3, (Red) sc 3, (Cream) sc 1. (15 sts)

Rnd 14: (Cream) sc 12, (Red) sc 2, (Cream) sc 1. (15 sts)

Rnd 15: (Cream) sc 1, (Red) sc 2, (Cream) sc 2, 4-dc bobble, sc 3, 4-dc bobble, sc 5. (15 sts)

Cont working in Cream only.

Stuff body firmly.

Rnd 16: dec 7 times, sc 1. (8 sts)

Fasten off, sew hole closed by pulling yarn tail through front loops of remaining sts.

Using Brown, embroider the eyes on head with straight stitch. Make 2 vertical lines on Rnd 6 for each eye, 4 sts apart.

Snout

Rnd 1: using Cream, sc 6 in a magic ring. (6 sts)

Fasten off invisibly, leaving long tail for sewing.

Using Brown, split yarn using only 2 strands, and embroider nostrils on snout. Make 1 vertical line for each nostril.

Sew snout between eyes on Rnds 7 and 8.

Using Mustard, cut a long strand to attach gold craft bell below head. Tie a bow on back to secure it. Tie a knot on both ends of strand to avoid splitting. Trim excess yarn.

Place cow souvenir inside backpack so Sully the Sloth can bring it home after his trip.

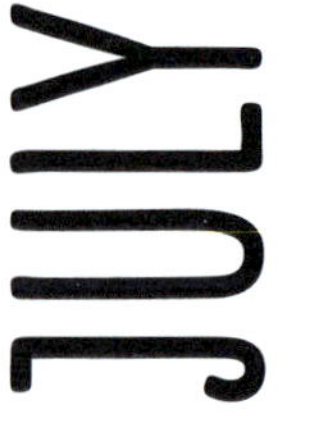

Gia Giraffe & Rory Rhino

July brings the full heat of summer, and the best way to enjoy the hot days is by having fun at the beach with Gia the Giraffe and Rory the Rhino. Gia the Giraffe loves to stay fresh with some ice cream and as for Rory the Rhino, he never goes to the beach without his favorite beach ball to play with in the sand.

GIA
13CM (5 1/8IN)

RORY
13CM (5 1/8IN)

PATTERN NOTES

Most pieces are worked in a spiral without joining each round. The tails and the beach towel are worked in turned rows.

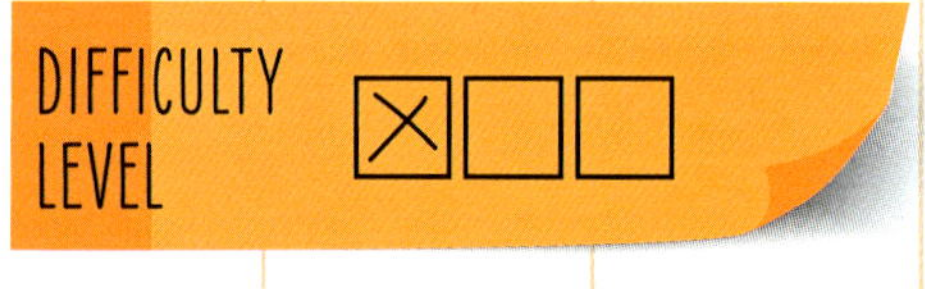

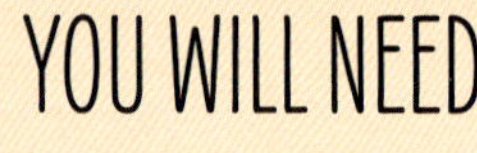

YOU WILL NEED

YARNS:

Hobbii Friends Cotton 8/4 (100% cotton) fingering (4-ply) weight, 160m (174yd) per 50g (1¾oz) ball, in the following shades:

FOR BOTH

- ✓ **Pale Pink:** 1 ball in Rose (44)

FOR GIA

- ✓ **Dark Yellow:** 1 ball in Dark Yellow (26)
- ✓ **Cream:** 1 ball in Oatmilk (03)
- ✓ **Dark Orange:** 1 ball in Whisky (16)
- ✓ **Light Blue:** 1 ball in Icy Blue (76)
- ✓ **Mid Green:** 1 ball in Misty Green (113)
- ✓ **Beige:** 1 ball in Dark Yellow (05)

FOR RORY

- ✓ **Pale Blue:** 1 ball in Baby Blue (75)
- ✓ **White:** 1 ball in White (01)
- ✓ **Yellow:** 1 ball in Sunflower (24)
- ✓ **Red:** 1 ball in Tomato (40)
- ✓ **Blue:** 1 ball in Aqua (91)

HOOK:

- ✓ 2.20mm (US B/1) crochet hook

TOOLS AND MATERIALS:

- ✓ 2 pairs of 8mm safety eyes
- ✓ Stitch markers
- ✓ Yarn needle
- ✓ Toy stuffing

Gia

Head

Rnd 1: using Dark Yellow, sc 6 in a magic ring. (6 sts)

Rnd 2: inc 6 times. (12 sts)

Rnd 3: [sc 1, inc] 6 times. (18 sts)

Rnd 4: [sc 2, inc] 6 times. (24 sts)

Rnd 5: [sc 3, inc] 6 times. (30 sts)

Rnd 6: [sc 4, inc] 6 times. (36 sts)

Rnd 7: [sc 5, inc] 6 times. (42 sts)

Rnd 8: [sc 6, inc] 6 times. (48 sts)

Rnds 9–12 (4 rnds): sc 1 in each st.

Rnd 13: [sc 7, inc] 6 times. (54 sts)

Rnds 14–19 (6 rnds): sc 1 in each st.

Rnd 20: [sc 7, dec] 6 times. (48 sts)

Rnd 21: [sc 6, dec] 6 times. (42 sts)

Rnd 22: [sc 5, dec] 6 times. (36 sts)

Place safety eyes between Rnds 14 and 15, 12 sts apart.

Start stuffing, cont as you work.

Rnd 23: [sc 4, dec] 6 times. (30 sts)

Rnd 24: [sc 3, dec] 6 times. (24 sts)

Rnd 25: [sc 2, dec] 6 times. (18 sts)

Rnd 26: [sc 1, dec] 6 times. (12 sts)

Rnd 27: dec 6 times. (6 sts)

Fasten off, sew hole closed by pulling yarn tail through front loops of remaining sts.

Muzzle

Rnd 1: using Cream, ch 6, start in 2nd ch from hook working in back bump of ch, sc 4, sc 3 in last ch, turn, cont on other side of ch (see Techniques: Crocheting Around Foundation Chain) working through both loops, sc 3, inc in last ch. (12 sts)

Rnd 2: inc, sc 3, inc 3 times, sc 3, inc twice. (18 sts)

Rnd 3: [sc 2, inc] 6 times. (24 sts)

Rnds 4–6 (3 rnds): sc 1 in each st.

Fasten off, leaving long tail for sewing.

Using Dark Orange, embroider nostrils on muzzle with straight stitch (see Techniques: Straight Stitch). Make 1 vertical line over Rnds 3 and 4 for each nostril, 6 sts apart. Then embroider a smile centered with nostrils on Rnd 2.

Sew muzzle to the head centered with eyes between Rnds 14 and 19. Stuff as you sew.

Cheeks (make 2)

Rnd 1: using Pale Pink, sc 6 in a magic ring. (6 sts)

Rnd 2: inc 6 times. (12 sts)

Fasten off invisibly, leave a long tail for sewing (see Techniques: Invisible Fasten Off).

Sew cheeks next to eyes between Rnds 15 and 18.

Horns (make 2)

Rnd 1: using Dark Orange, sc 6 in a magic ring. (6 sts)

Rnd 2: inc 6 times. (12 sts)

Rnds 3 and 4 (2 rnds): sc 1 in each st.

Rnd 5: [sc 1, dec] 4 times. (8 sts)

Rnds 6–8 (3 rnds): change to Dark Yellow, sc 1 in each st.

Fasten off, leaving long tail for sewing.

Stuff horns firmly. Sew horns on each side of head between Rnds 5 and 7.

Ears (make 2)

Rnd 1: using Dark Yellow, sc 6 in a magic ring. (6 sts)

Rnd 2: [sc 1, inc] 3 times. (9 sts)

Rnd 3: sc 1 in each st.

Rnd 4: [sc 2, inc] 3 times. (12 sts)

Rnds 5 and 6 (2 rnds): sc 1 in each st.

Rnd 7: [sc 1, dec] 4 times. (8 sts)

Do not stuff. Flatten opening and work next row through both layers to close (see Techniques: Closing with Single Crochet).

Row 8: sc 4. (4 sts)

Fasten off, leaving long tail for sewing.

Flatten ears in opposite direction of last rnd. Sew ears below horns, between Rnds 7 and 8.

Small spot

Rnd 1: using Dark Orange, sc 6 in a magic ring. (6 sts)

Fasten off invisibly, leaving long tail for sewing.

Large spot

Rnd 1: using Dark Orange, hdc 8 in a magic ring. (8 sts)

Fasten off invisibly, leaving long tail for sewing.

Sew spots to front of head.

Body

Rnd 1: using Light Blue, sc 6 in a magic ring. (6 sts)

Rnd 2: inc 6 times. (12 sts)

Rnd 3: [sc 1, inc] 6 times. (18 sts)

Rnd 4: [sc 2, inc] 6 times. (24 sts)

Rnd 5: [sc 3, inc] 6 times. (30 sts)

Rnd 6: [sc 4, inc] 6 times. (36 sts)

Rnd 7: [sc 5, inc] 6 times. (42 sts)

Rnd 8: [sc 6, inc] 6 times. (48 sts)

Rnds 9–12 (4 rnds): sc 1 in each st.

Rnd 13: working in BLO, sc 1 in each st.

Rnd 14: [sc 7, dec, sc 7] 3 times. (45 sts)

Rnds 15 and 16 (2 rnds): change to Pale Pink, sc 1 in each st.

Start stuffing, cont as you work.

Rnd 17: change to Light Blue, [sc 13, dec] 3 times. (42 sts)

Rnd 18: sc 1 in each st.

Rnd 19: change to Pale Pink, sc 1 in each st.

Rnd 20: [sc 6, dec, sc 6] 3 times. (39 sts)

Rnd 21: change to Light Blue, sc 1 in each st.

Rnd 22: [sc 11, dec] 3 times. (36 sts)

Rnd 23: change to Dark Yellow, working in BLO, sc 1 in each st.

Rnd 24: [sc 4, dec] 6 times. (30 sts)

Rnd 25: [sc 3, dec] 6 times. (24 sts)

Rnds 26–28 (3 rnds): sc 1 in each st.

Fasten off, leaving long tail for sewing.

SWIMSUIT SKIRT

Using Pale Pink, hold body upside down and join yarn to first unworked loop of Rnd 12 with slst 1 (does not count as a st) (see Techniques: Joining Yarn to Add a Detail). Start next rnd in same st.

Rnd 1: inc in each st. (96 sts)

Rnds 2 and 3 (2 rnds): sc 1 in each st.

Fasten off invisibly and weave in yarn ends.

SWIMSUIT DETAIL

Hold body upside down and join Light Blue to first unworked loop of Rnd 22 with slst 1 (counts as first st of next rnd).

Rnd 1: slst 1 in each st. (36 sts)

Fasten off invisibly and weave in yarn ends.

Sew body to bottom of head.

Legs (make 2)

Rnd 1: using Dark Orange, sc 6 in a magic ring. (6 sts)

Rnd 2: inc 6 times. (12 sts)

Rnds 3–5 (3 rnds): sc 1 in each st.

Rnds 6 and 7 (2 rnds): change to Dark Yellow, sc 1 in each st.

Rnd 8: [sc 3, inc] 3 times. (15 sts)

Rnds 9–11 (3 rnds): sc 1 in each st.

Fasten off, leaving long tail for sewing.

Stuff firmly. Sew legs to body between Rnds 7 and 11, 7 sts apart. Gia the Giraffe should be able to sit on a flat surface.

Arms (make 2)

Rnd 1: using Dark Orange, sc 6 in a magic ring. (6 sts)

Rnd 2: [sc 1, inc] 3 times. (9 sts)

Rnds 3 and 4 (2 rnds): sc 1 in each st.

Rnds 5–12 (8 rnds): change to Dark Yellow, sc 1 in each st.

Stuff lightly. Flatten opening and work next row through both layers to close.

Row 13: sc 4, leave 1 st unworked. (4 sts)

Fasten off, leaving long tail for sewing.

Sew arms on each side of body between Rnds 24 and 25.

Swimsuit straps (make 2)

Using Pale Pink, cut 1 strand of 20cm (8in) for each swimsuit strap.

Run strand through two sts of swimsuit detail, one on each side of arm. Make a loop above arm and tie a knot with a bow to secure it. Tie a knot on both ends of strand to avoid splitting. Trim excess yarn (see Photo 1).

Tail

Row 1: using Dark Yellow, ch 7, starting in 2nd ch from hook, slst 6. (6 sts)

Fasten off, leaving long tail for sewing.

Using Dark Orange, cut 2 strands of 5cm (2in). Attach strands to tip of tail (see Techniques: Attaching Yarn Strands). Split strands for texture. Trim to desired length.

Sew tail to back of body on Rnd 8 (see Photo 2).

28	29	30
		International Friendship Day

Ice cream

Start by making scoop and cone separately.

SCOOP

Rnd 1: using Mid Green, sc 6 in a magic ring. (6 sts)

Rnd 2: inc 6 times. (12 sts)

Rnd 3: [sc 1, inc] 6 times. (18 sts)

Rnds 4–6 (3 rnds): sc 1 in each st.

Rnd 7: [sc 2, dec, sc 2] 3 times. (15 sts)

Rnd 8: working in FLO, [hdc 2 in same st, slst 1] 7 times, slst 1. (22 sts)

Fasten off and weave in yarn end.

Stuff firmly.

Using Pale Pink, embroider sprinkles on scoop.

CONE

Rnd 1: using Beige, sc 6 in a magic ring. (6 sts)

Rnd 2: sc 1 in each st.

Rnd 3: [sc 1, inc] 3 times. (9 sts)

Rnd 4: sc 1 in each st.

Rnd 5: [sc 1, inc, sc 1] 3 times. (12 sts)

Rnd 6: sc 1 in each st.

Rnd 7: [sc 3, inc] 3 times. (15 sts)

Fasten off, leaving long tail for sewing.

Stuff firmly.

Sew last rnd of cone to unworked loops of Rnd 7 of scoop. Add more stuffing before completely closing.

Beach towel

Row 1: using Cream, ch 22, start in 2nd ch from hook working in back bump of ch, [sc 1, ch 1 and skip next ch] 10 times, sc 1 in last ch (see Photo 3), turn. (11 sts + 10 chs)

Row 2: ch 1, [sc 1 in ch-1 sp, ch 1] 10 times (see Photos 4 and 5), sc 1 in last st, turn. (11 sts + 10 chs)

Rows 3 and 4 (2 rows): change to Mid Green, rep Row 2.

Rows 5 and 6 (2 rows): change to Cream, rep Row 2.

Rows 7–30 (24 rows): rep Rows 3 to 6 six more times. (11 sts + 10 chs)

Fasten off and weave in yarn ends.

Using Mid Green, cut 22 strands of 5cm (2in). Attach strands on short sides of beach towel (11 strands on each side). Trim to desired length.

3

4

5

Rory

Head

Rnd 1: using Pale Blue, sc 8 in a magic ring. (8 sts)

Rnd 2: inc 8 times. (16 sts)

Rnd 3: [sc 1, inc] 8 times. (24 sts)

Rnd 4: [sc 2, inc] 8 times. (32 sts)

Rnds 5 and 6 (2 rnds): sc 1 in each st.

Rnd 7: [sc 10, 4-dc bobble (see Techniques: Bobble Stitch)] twice, sc 10. (32 sts)

Rnd 8: sc 1 in each st.

Rnd 9: [sc 7, inc] 4 times. (36 sts)

Rnd 10: [sc 4, inc, sc 4] 4 times. (40 sts)

Rnd 11: sc 1 in each st.

Rnd 12: sc 12, [inc, sc 4] 4 times, sc 8. (44 sts)

Rnd 13: sc 13, [inc, sc 5] 4 times, sc 7. (48 sts)

Rnd 14: sc 1 in each st.

Rnd 15: sc 7, [inc, sc 6] 5 times, inc, sc 5. (54 sts)

Rnd 16: sc 1 in each st.

Rnd 17: [sc 7, inc] 6 times, sc 6. (60 sts)

Rnds 18–27 (10 rnds): sc 1 in each st.

Place safety eyes between Rnds 13 and 14, 16 sts apart. Eyes should be aligned with nostrils (see Photo 2).

Start stuffing, cont as you work.

Rnd 28: [sc 8, dec] 6 times. (54 sts)

Rnd 29: [sc 7, dec] 6 times. (48 sts)

Rnd 30: [sc 6, dec] 6 times. (42 sts)

Rnd 31: [sc 5, dec] 6 times. (36 sts)

Rnd 32: [sc 4, dec] 6 times. (30 sts)

Rnd 33: [sc 3, dec] 6 times. (24 sts)

Rnd 34: [sc 2, dec] 6 times. (18 sts)

Rnd 35: [sc 1, dec] 6 times. (12 sts)

Rnd 36: dec 6 times. (6 sts)

Fasten off, sew hole closed by pulling yarn tail through front loops of remaining sts.

Using White, embroider smile on front of head (see Photo 3) in straight stitch (see Techniques: Straight Stitch.

Cheeks (make 2)

Rnd 1: using Pale Pink, sc 6 in a magic ring. (6 sts)

Rnd 2: inc 6 times. (12 sts)

Fasten off invisibly, leaving long tail for sewing (see Techniques: Invisible Fasten Off).

Sew cheeks next to eyes between Rnds 15 and 18 (see Photo 2).

Ears (make 2)

Start by making inner layer and outer layer of ears separately.

INNER LAYERS (MAKE 1 FOR EACH EAR)

Rnd 1: using Pale Pink, sc 6 in a magic ring. (6 sts)

Rnd 2: inc 6 times. (12 sts)

Rnd 3: [sc 1, inc] 6 times. (18 sts)

Fasten off. Set aside.

OUTER LAYERS (MAKE 1 FOR EACH EAR)

Rnd 1: using Pale Blue, sc 6 in a magic ring. (6 sts)

Rnd 2: inc 6 times. (12 sts)

Rnd 3: [sc 1, inc] 6 times. (18 sts)

Align sts of outer layer with inner layer (wrong sides together) and work next rnd through both layers.

Rnd 4: sc 1 in each st.

Fasten off, leaving long tail for sewing.

Fold bottom of ear and with yarn tail sew sides together to shape ear (see Photo 1).

Sew ears to top of head over Rnds 24 and 25, 12 sts apart (see Photo 3).

Hair tuft

Row 1: using Pale Blue, ch 4, starting in 2nd ch from hook, slst 3, ch 5, starting in 2nd ch from hook, slst 4, ch 4, starting in 2nd ch from hook, slst 3. (3 hair strands)

Fasten off, leaving long tail for sewing.

Sew hair tuft to top of head, between ears, on Rnd 24, (see Photos 2 and 3).

Large horn

Rnd 1: using White, sc 6 in a magic ring. (6 sts)

Rnd 2: [sc 1, inc] 3 times. (9 sts)

Rnd 3: sc 1 in each st.

Rnd 4: [sc 1, inc, sc 1] 3 times. (12 sts)

Rnd 5: sc 1 in each st.

Rnd 6: [sc 3, inc] 3 times. (15 sts)

Rnd 7: sc 1 in each st.

Fasten off, leaving long tail for sewing.

Stuff firmly.

Sew large horn centered with nostrils, between Rnds 4 and 8 (see Photos 2 and 3).

Small horn

Work as for large horn for Rnds 1–3.

Fasten off, leaving long tail for sewing.

Stuff firmly.

Sew small horn aligned with large horn, between Rnds 12 and 14 (see Photo 2).

Legs and body

LEG 1

Rnd 1: using Pale Blue, sc 8 in a magic ring. (8 sts)

Rnd 2: inc 8 times. (16 sts)

Cont alternating from Pale Blue to White to make toes.

Rnd 3: working in BLO, [(Pale Blue) sc 1, (White) 3-hdc puff (see Techniques: Puff Stitch)] 3 times, (Pale Blue) sc 10. (16 sts)

Cont working in Pale Blue only.

Rnd 4: sc 1 in each st.

Rnd 5: [sc 7, inc] twice. (18 sts)

Rnds 6–10 (5 rnds): sc 1 in each st.

Fasten off. Set aside.

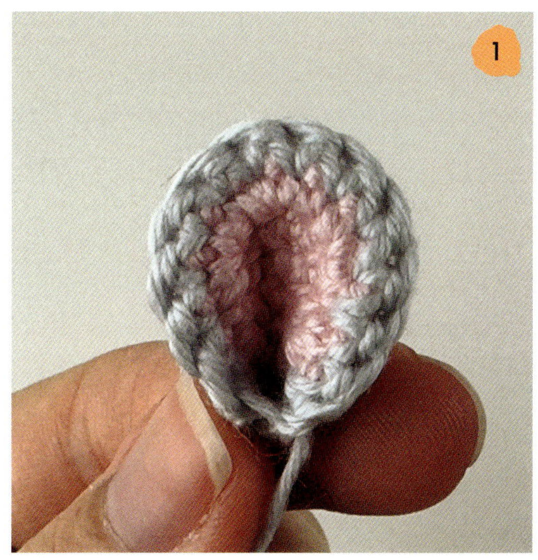

LEG 2

Work as for leg 1, but do not fasten off at end. Cont working on body.

BODY

Rnd 11: still with leg 2 on hook, ch 2, sc 1 in 10th st of leg 1 to join (see Techniques: Joining Legs), PM here for new beg of rnd, sc 1 in each st of leg 1, inc in each ch, sc 1 in each st of leg 2, inc in each ch. (44 sts)

Rnds 12 and 13 (2 rnds): sc 1 in each st.

Stuff legs firmly.

Rnd 14: [sc 8, inc, sc 2] 4 times. (48 sts)

Rnds 15–19 (5 rnds): sc 1 in each st.

Rnd 20: [sc 7, dec, sc 7] 3 times. (45 sts)

Rnds 21 and 22 (2 rnds): sc 1 in each st.

Rnd 23: [sc 13, dec] 3 times. (42 sts)

Rnds 24 and 25 (2 rnds): sc 1 in each st.

Rnd 26: [sc 6, dec, sc 6] 3 times. (39 sts)

Rnd 27: sc 1 in each st.

Rnd 28: [sc 11, dec] 3 times. (36 sts)

Rnd 29: sc 1 in each st.

Rnd 30: [sc 5, dec, sc 5] 3 times. (33 sts)

Rnd 31: [sc 9, dec] 3 times. (30 sts)

Fasten off, leaving long tail for sewing.

Stuff body firmly.

Sew body to bottom of head between Rnds 16 and 26.

Arms (make 2)

Rnd 1: using Pale Blue, sc 6 in a magic ring. (6 sts)

Rnd 2: inc 6 times. (12 sts)

Rnds 3–16 (14 rnds): sc 1 in each st.

Stuff lightly. Flatten opening, work next row through both layers to close (see Techniques: Closing with Single Crochet).

Row 17: sc 6. (6 sts)

Fasten off, leaving long tail for sewing.

Sew arms on each side of body between Rnds 30 and 31.

Tail

Row 1: using Pale Blue, ch 7, starting in 2nd ch from hook, slst 6. (6 sts)

Fasten off, leaving long tail for sewing.

Using Pale Blue, cut two strands 5cm (2in) each. Attach strands to tip of tail (see Techniques: Attaching Yarn Strands). Split strands for texture. Trim to desired length (see Photo 4).

Sew tail to back of the body on Rnd 15.

Swim shorts

Start by making legs of swim shorts.

SWIM SHORT LEG 1

Using Yellow, ch 21, join to first ch on back bump with slst 1 to make a chain ring. Ch 1, start next rnd in same st.

Rnd 1: sc 1 in each back bump of ch. (21 sts)

Rnd 2: [sc 1, spike sc (see Techniques: Spike Single Crochet)] 10 times, sc 1. (21 sts)

Rnd 3: [spike sc, sc 1] 10 times, spike sc (21 sts)

Fasten off. Set aside.

SWIM SHORT LEG 2

Work as for swim short leg 1, but do not fasten off at end. Cont working with shorts.

JOINING THE LEGS

Rnd 4: still with leg 2 on hook, ch 1, sc 1 in first st of leg 1 to join, PM here for new beg of rnd, [spike sc, sc 1] 10 times on leg 1, sc 1 on ch, [sc 1, spike sc] 10 times on leg 2, sc 1, inc on ch. (45 sts)

Rnd 5: [spike sc, sc 1] twice, spike sc. (45 sts)

Rnd 6: [sc 1, spike sc] twice, sc 1. (45 sts)

Rnds 7–10 (4 rnds): rep Rnds 5 and 6 twice more.

IF NECESSARY, ADJUST THE POSITION OF THE CHAIN FOR THE HOLE FOR THE TAIL, MAKING SURE IT'S CENTERED AT THE BACK OF THE SWIM SHORTS.

Rnd 11: [spike sc, sc 1] 21 times, spike sc, ch 2 and skip 2 sts. (43 sts + 2 chs)

Rnd 12: [sc 1, spike sc] 21 times, sc 1, sc 1 in each ch. (45 sts)

Rnd 13: [spike sc, sc 1] 5 times, end rnd here. (10 sts)

Rnd 14: sc 1 in each st. (45 sts)

Fasten off invisibly and weave in yarn ends.

Place swim shorts on Rory the Rhino with tail going through the gap from Rnd 11 (see Photo 4).

Beach ball

Rnd 1: using White, sc 6 in a magic ring. (6 sts)

Cont alternating from White, to Yellow, Red, and Blue to make stripes.

Rnd 2: (White) inc, (Yellow) inc, (White) inc, (Red) inc, (White) inc, (Blue) inc. (12 sts)

Rnd 3: (White) sc 1, inc, (Yellow) sc 1, inc, (White) sc 1, inc, (Red) sc 1, inc, (White) sc 1, inc, (Blue) sc 1, inc. (18 sts)

Rnd 4: (White) sc 1, inc, sc 1, (Yellow) sc 1, inc, sc 1, (White) sc 1, inc, sc 1, (Red) sc 1, inc, sc 1, (White) sc 1, inc, sc 1, (Blue) sc 1, inc, sc 1. (24 sts)

Rnd 5: (White) sc 3, inc, (Yellow) sc 3, inc, (White) sc 3, inc, (Red) sc 3, inc, (White) sc 3, inc, (Blue) sc 3, inc. (30 sts)

Rnds 6–11 (6 rnds): (White) sc 5, (Yellow) sc 5, (White) sc 5, (Red) sc 5, (White) sc 5, (Blue) sc 5. (30 sts)

Start stuffing, cont as you work.

Rnd 12: (White) sc 3, dec, (Yellow) sc 3, dec, (White) sc 3, dec, (Red) sc 3, dec, (White) sc 3, dec, (Blue) sc 3, dec. (24 sts)

Rnd 13: (White) sc 1, dec, sc 1, (Yellow) sc 1, dec, sc 1, (White) sc 1, dec, sc 1, (Red) sc 1, dec, sc 1, (White) sc 1, dec, sc 1, (Blue) sc 1, dec, sc 1. (18 sts)

Rnd 14: (White) sc 1, dec, (Yellow) sc 1, dec, (White) sc 1, dec, (Red) sc 1, dec, (White) sc 1, dec, (Blue) sc 1, dec. (12 sts)

Cont working in White only.

Rnd 15: dec 6 times. (6 sts)

Fasten off, sew hole closed by pulling yarn tail through front loops of remaining sts (see Photo 5).

4

5

AUGUST

Cassia Capybara & Camomile Cow

It's a beautiful day at the farmer's market, with vendors showing off their best crops. Cassia runs a citrus stand, selling the juiciest oranges in the market, while Camomile is best known for her beautiful flowers, perfect to gift for any special occasion.

CASSIA
14.5CM (5¾IN)

CAMOMILE
14.5CM (5¾IN)

PATTERN NOTES

Most pieces are worked in a spiral without joining each round. The front and back panels of the dress and the apron are worked in rows.

DIFFICULTY LEVEL

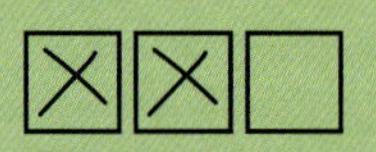

YOU WILL NEED

YARNS:

Hobbii Friends Cotton 8/4 (100% cotton) fingering (4-ply) weight, 160m (174yd) per 50g (1¾oz) ball, in the following shades:

FOR BOTH

- ✓ **Dark Brown:** 1 ball in Chestnut (11)
- ✓ **Pale Pink:** 1 ball in Rose (44)
- ✓ **White:** 1 ball in White (01)
- ✓ **Orange:** 1 ball in Peach (33)

FOR CASSIA

- ✓ **Caramel:** 1 ball in Caramel (14)
- ✓ **Dark Gray:** small amount in Charcoal (123)
- ✓ **Dark Green:** 1 ball in Hunter Green (116)
- ✓ **Olive:** 1 ball in Olive (109)

FOR CAMOMILE

- ✓ **Cream:** 1 ball in Oatmilk (03)
- ✓ **Light Brown:** 1 ball in Nougat (09)
- ✓ **Sage:** 1 ball in Sage (114)
- ✓ **Beige:** 1 ball in Beige (05)
- ✓ **Yellow Green:** small amount in Pistachio (108)
- ✓ **Yellow:** small amount in Sunflower (24)

HOOK:

- ✓ 2.20mm (US B/1) crochet hook

TOOLS AND MATERIALS:

- ✓ 2 pairs of 8mm safety eyes
- ✓ Stitch markers
- ✓ Yarn needle
- ✓ Toy stuffing
- ✓ Gold craft bell
- ✓ Craft chenille stems (pipe cleaners) or craft wire

Cassia

Head

Rnd 1: using Caramel, sc 6 in a magic ring. (6 sts)

Rnd 2: inc 6 times. (12 sts)

Rnd 3: [sc 1, inc] 6 times. (18 sts)

Rnd 4: [sc 2, inc] 6 times. (24 sts)

Rnd 5: [sc 3, inc] 6 times. (30 sts)

Rnd 6: [sc 4, inc] 6 times. (36 sts)

Rnd 7: [sc 5, inc] 6 times. (42 sts)

Rnd 8: [sc 13, inc] 3 times. (45 sts)

Rnds 9–11 (3 rnds): sc 1 in each st.

Rnd 12: [sc 7, inc, sc 7] 3 times. (48 sts)

Rnds 13–15 (3 rnds): sc 1 in each st.

Rnd 16: [sc 7, inc] 6 times. (54 sts)

Rnds 17–21 (5 rnds): sc 1 in each st.

Rnd 22: [sc 7, dec] 6 times. (48 sts)

Rnd 23: [sc 6, dec] 6 times. (42 sts)

Rnd 24: [sc 5, dec] 6 times. (36 sts)

Place safety eyes between Rnds 14 and 15, 12 sts apart.

Start stuffing, cont as you work.

Rnd 25: [sc 4, dec] 6 times. (30 sts)

Rnd 26: [sc 3, dec] 6 times. (24 sts)

Rnd 27: [sc 2, dec] 6 times. (18 sts)

Rnd 28: [sc 1, dec] 6 times. (12 sts)

Rnd 29: dec 6 times. (6 sts)

Fasten off, sew hole closed by pulling yarn tail through front loops of remaining sts.

Using Caramel, embroider eyelids in straight stitch (see Techniques: Straight Stitch). Make 3 diagonal lines over each eye 2 sts wide.

Muzzle

Rnd 1: using Dark Brown, ch 6, start in 2nd ch from hook working in back bump of ch, sc 4, sc 3 in last ch, turn, cont on other side of ch (see Techniques: Crocheting Around Foundation Chain) working through both loops, sc 3, inc in last ch. (12 sts)

Rnd 2: [sc 3 in same st, sc 3, sc 3 in same st, sc 1] twice. (20 sts)

Rnd 3: [sc 1, sc 3 in same st, sc 5, sc 3 in same st, sc 2] twice. (28 sts)

Rnds 4–6 (3 rnds): sc 1 in each st. (28 sts)

Fasten off, leaving long tail for sewing.

Using Dark Gray, embroider nose on muzzle in straight stitch. Make a vertical line over foundation chain of Rnd 1, then a "V" at top over Rnds 2–4.

Sew muzzle to the head centered with eyes between Rnds 12 and 22. Stuff as you sew.

Cheeks (make 2)

Rnd 1: using Pale Pink, sc 6 in a magic ring. (6 sts)

Rnd 2: inc 6 times. (12 sts)

Fasten off invisibly, leaving long tail for sewing (see Techniques: Invisible Fasten Off).

Sew cheeks next to eyes between Rnds 15 and 18.

Ears (make 2)

Rnd 1: using Caramel, sc 6 in a magic ring. (6 sts)

Rnd 2: [sc 1, inc] 3 times. (9 sts)

Rnds 3 and 4 (2 rnds): sc 1 in each st.

Do not stuff. Flatten ear, pinch sides of opening and, with yarn tail, sew sides together to shape ear.

Sew ears to top of head over Rnds 7 and 8.

Legs and body

LEG 1

Rnd 1: using Dark Brown, sc 6 in a magic ring. (6 sts)

Rnd 2: inc 6 times. (12 sts)

Rnds 3–7 (5 rnds): sc 1 in each st.

Rnds 8–12 (5 rnds): change to Caramel, sc 1 in each st.

Fasten off. Set aside.

LEG 2

Work as for leg 1, but do not fasten off at end. Cont working on body.

IF NECESSARY, ADD A FEW MORE STITCHES ON LEG 2 TO SHIFT THE COLOR CHANGE TO THE BACK OF THE LEG.

BODY

Rnd 13: still with leg 2 on hook, ch 3, sc 1 in last st of leg 1 to join (see Techniques: Joining Legs), PM here for new beg of rnd, sc 1 in each st of leg 1, inc in each ch, sc 1 in each st of leg 2, inc in each ch. (36 sts)

Stuff legs firmly.

Rnds 14–18 (5 rnds): sc 1 in each st.

Rnd 19: change to Dark Green, slst 1 in each st loosely.

Rnd 20: working in BLO of Rnd 19 and both loops of Rnd 18 (see Techniques: Straight Stripe Color Change), sc 1 in each st. (36 sts)

Rnd 21: [sc 5, dec, sc 5] 3 times. (33 sts)

Rnds 22 and 23 (2 rnds): sc 1 in each st.

Rnd 24: [sc 9, dec] 3 times. (30 sts)

Rnds 25 and 26 (2 rnds): sc 1 in each st.

Rnd 27: [sc 4, dec, sc 4] 3 times. (27 sts)

Rnds 28 and 29 (2 rnds): sc 1 in each st.

Rnd 30: [sc 7, dec] 3 times, turn. (24 sts)

Cont working in opposite direction.

IF NECESSARY, ADJUST THE POSITION OF THE COLLAR'S SPLIT TO ALIGN WITH THE GAP BETWEEN THE LEGS.

Rnd 31: ch 2, working in BLO, dc 11, ch 3, slst 1, ch 3, dc 12, slst 1 to first st to join. (24 sts)

Fasten off, leaving long tail for sewing.

Stuff body firmly.

SHIRT HEM DETAIL

Hold body with legs up and join Dark Green to first unworked loop of Rnd 19 with slst 1 (counts as first st of next rnd).

Rnd 1: slst 1 in each st. (36 sts)

Fasten off invisibly and weave in yarn ends.

Sew body to bottom of head using unworked loops from Rnd 30.

Arms (make 2)

Rnd 1: using Dark Brown, sc 6 in a magic ring. (6 sts)

Rnd 2: [sc 1, inc] 3 times. (9 sts)

Rnds 3–6 (4 rnds): sc 1 in each st.

Rnd 7: change to Dark Green, slst 1 in each st loosely.

Rnd 8: working in BLO of Rnd 7 and both loops of Rnd 6, sc 1 in each st. (9 sts)

Rnds 9–15 (7 rnds): sc 1 in each st.

Stuff lightly. Flatten opening and work next row through both layers to close (see Techniques: Closing with Single Crochet).

Row 16: sc 4, leave 1 st unworked. (4 sts)

Fasten off, leaving long tail for sewing.

SHIRT CUFF DETAIL

Hold arm with hand up and join Dark Green to first unworked loop of Rnd 7 with slst 1 (does not count as a st). Start next rnd in next st.

Rnd 1: [ch 2, slst 1] 9 times. (9 sts + 18 chs)

Fasten off invisibly and weave in yarn ends.

Sew arms on each side of body between Rnds 29 and 30.

Dress

Start by making front and back panels, which are joined to make skirt, and pocket separately.

FRONT PANEL

Row 1: using Olive, ch 9, start in 2nd ch from hook working in back bump of ch, sc 8, turn. (8 sts)

Rows 2 and 3 (2 rows): ch 1, sc 8, turn. (8 sts)

Row 4: ch 1, sc 8. (8 sts)

Fasten off and weave in yarn ends.

BACK PANEL

Work as for Front panel, but do not fasten off at end. Cont working on skirt.

SKIRT

Rnd 5: still with back panel on hook, ch 10, PM in first ch for new beg of rnd, sc 1 in first st of Row 4 of front panel, sc 7 on front panel, ch 10, sc 1 in first st of Row 4 of back panel, sc 7 on back panel (see Photos 1 and 2). (16 sts + 20 chs)

Rnd 6: [sc 1 in each ch, sc 8] twice. (36 sts)

Rnd 7: [sc 4, inc, sc 4] 4 times. (40 sts)

Rnds 8–11 (4 rnds): sc 1 in each st.

Rnd 12: [sc 9, inc] 4 times. (44 sts)

Rnds 13 and 14 (2 rnds): sc 1 in each st.

DO NOT CUT OLIVE, LEAVE YARN AT THE FRONT OF THE WORK.

Rnd 15: change to White, working in BLO, sc 1 in each st.

Rnd 16: [ch 2, slst 1] 44 times. (44 sts + 88 chs)

Fasten off and weave in yarn ends.

Go back to Olive on Rnd 14. Insert hook in unworked loop next to yarn and pull up a loop (see Photo 3). Start next rnd in next st.

Rnd 15: sc 1 in each st. (44 sts)

Fasten off invisibly and weave in yarn ends.

DRESS OPENING DETAIL

Using Olive, make a slip knot on hook. Start next rnd in top right corner of back panel, through both loops of foundation chain, and work all around opening of dress.

Rnd 1: sc 8 on foundation ch, ch 1, sc 5 on side of rows, sc 10 on ch, sc 5 on side of rows, ch 1, sc 8 on foundation ch, ch 1, sc 5 on side of rows, sc 10 on ch, sc 5 on side of rows, ch 1. (56 sts + 4 chs)

Fasten off invisibly and weave in yarn ends.

POCKET

Row 1: using Olive, ch 4, start in 2nd ch from hook working in back bump of ch, inc 3 times, turn. (6 sts)

Row 2: ch 1, sc 6. (6 sts)

Cont working around pocket.

Row 3: ch 1, sc 2 on side of rows, sc 3 on foundation ch, sc 2 on side of rows, ch 1. (7 sts + 2 chs)

Fasten off invisibly, leaving long tail for sewing.

Sew pocket to front panel of dress, leaving top open.

Using White, Dark Green, and Orange, embroider flower details on bottom part of the dress (see Photo 4).

DRESS STRAPS (MAKE 2)

Using Olive, cut 1 strand of 20cm (8in) for each dress strap.

Run strand through corner chains of front and back panels of dress on each side making a loop.

Place dress on Cassia the Capybara with straps over arms and tie a knot with a bow to secure. Tie a knot on both ends of strand to avoid splitting. Trim excess yarn.

Basket

Rnd 1: using Dark Brown, ch 7, start in 2nd ch from hook working in back bump of ch, inc, sc 4, sc 4 in last ch, turn, cont on other side of ch working through both loops, sc 4, inc in last ch. (16 sts)

Rnd 2: [inc twice, sc 4, inc twice] twice. (24 sts)

Rnd 3: [sc 1, inc twice, sc 6, inc twice, sc 1] twice. (32 sts)

Rnd 4: working in BLO, sc 31, inc. (33 sts)

Rnd 5: [spike sc (see Techniques: Spike Single Crochet), sc 1 BLO] 16 times, spike sc. (33 sts)

Rnd 6: [sc 1 BLO, spike st] 16 times, sc 1 BLO. (33 sts)

Rnds 7–14 (8 rnds): rep Rnds 5 and 6 four more times.

Basket straps are worked in next rnd.

Rnd 15: slst 5, ch 24, join with slst 1 to an unworked loop of Rnd 3 aligned with top of ch (see Photo 5), ch 1 and turn, slst 24 on ch, cont working on basket, slst 7, ch 24, join with slst 1 to an unworked loop of Rnd 3 aligned with top of ch, ch 1 and turn, slst 24 on ch, cont working on basket, slst 21. (33 sts + 2 straps)

Fasten off and weave in yarn ends.

Oranges (make 3)

Start by making fruit and leaf separately.

FRUIT (MAKE 1 FOR EACH ORANGE)

Rnd 1: using Orange, sc 6 in a magic ring. (6 sts)

Rnd 2: inc 6 times. (12 sts)

Rnd 3: [sc 1, inc] 6 times. (18 sts)

Rnds 4–7 (4 rnds): sc 1 in each st.

Rnd 8: [sc 1, dec] 6 times. (12 sts)

Stuff firmly.

Rnd 9: dec 6 times. (6 sts)

Fasten off, sew hole closed by pulling yarn tail through front loops of remaining sts.

LEAVES (MAKE 1 FOR EACH ORANGE)

Row 1: using Olive, ch 4, starting in 2nd ch from hook, slst 1, sc 1, slst 1. (3 sts)

Fasten off, leaving long tail for sewing.

Sew leaf to top of the fruit.

Place oranges inside basket or on Cassia the Capybara's head. Place basket on Cassia the Capybara's back with straps over arms.

Camomile

Head

Rnd 1: using Cream, sc 6 in a magic ring. (6 sts)

Rnd 2: inc 6 times. (12 sts)

Cont alternating from Cream to Light Brown to make head patch.

Rnd 3: (Cream) [sc 1, inc] 3 times, sc 1, (Light Brown) inc, sc 1, inc, (Cream) sc 1, inc. (18 sts)

Rnd 4: (Cream) [sc 2, inc] 3 times, sc 1, (Light Brown) sc 1, inc, sc 2, inc, (Cream) sc 2, inc. (24 sts)

Rnd 5: (Cream) [sc 3, inc] 3 times, sc 1, (Light Brown) sc 2, inc, sc 3, inc, (Cream) sc 3, inc. (30 sts)

Rnd 6: (Cream) [sc 4, inc] 3 times, sc 1, (Light Brown) sc 3, inc, sc 4, inc, (Cream) sc 4, inc. (36 sts)

Rnd 7: (Cream) [sc 5, inc] 3 times, sc 2, (Light Brown) sc 3, inc, sc 5, inc, (Cream) sc 5, inc. (42 sts)

Rnd 8: (Cream) [sc 6, inc] 3 times, sc 2, (Light Brown) sc 4, inc, sc 6, inc, (Cream) sc 6, inc. (48 sts)

Rnd 9: (Cream) sc 11, (Light Brown) sc 3, (Cream) sc 1, inc, sc 11, (Light Brown) sc 4, inc, sc 8, (Cream) sc 7, inc. (51 sts)

Rnd 10: (Cream) sc 10, (Light Brown) sc 5, (Cream) sc 13, (Light Brown) sc 14, (Cream) sc 9. (51 sts)

Rnd 11: (Cream) sc 7, (Light Brown) sc 8, (Cream) sc 14, (Light Brown) sc 12, (Cream) sc 10. (51 sts)

Rnd 12: (Cream) sc 6, (Light Brown) sc 8, (Cream) sc 15, (Light Brown) sc 12, (Cream) sc 10. (51 sts)

Rnd 13: (Cream) sc 6, (Light Brown) sc 8, (Cream) sc 2, inc, sc 15, (Light Brown) sc 1, inc, sc 5, (Cream) sc 11, inc. (54 sts)

Rnd 14: (Cream) sc 8, (Light Brown) sc 5, (Cream) sc 21, Light Brown) sc 5, (Cream) sc 15. (54 sts)

Rnd 15: (Cream) sc 10, (Light Brown) sc 2, (Cream) sc 23, (Light Brown) sc 3, (Cream) sc 16. (54 sts)

Cont working in Cream only.

Rnds 16–21 (6 rnds): sc 1 in each st.

Rnd 22: [sc 7, dec] 6 times. (48 sts)

Rnd 23: [sc 6, dec] 6 times. (42 sts)

Rnd 24: [sc 5, dec] 6 times. (36 sts)

Place safety eyes between Rnds 15 and 16, 12 sts apart. First eye should be between 19th and 20th sts, and 2nd between 31st and 32nd sts.

Start stuffing, cont as you work.

Rnd 25: [sc 4, dec] 6 times. (30 sts)

Rnd 26: [sc 3, dec] 6 times. (24 sts)

Rnd 27: [sc 2, dec] 6 times. (18 sts)

Rnd 28: [sc 1, dec] 6 times. (12 sts)

Rnd 29: dec 6 times. (6 sts)

Fasten off, sew hole closed by pulling yarn tail through front loops of remaining sts.

Muzzle

Rnd 1: using Pale Pink, ch 6, start in 2nd ch from hook working in back bump of ch, sc 4, sc 3 in last ch, turn, cont on other side of ch (see Techniques: Crocheting Around Foundation Chain) working through both loops, sc 3, inc in last ch. (12 sts)

Rnd 2: inc, sc 3, inc 3 times, sc 3, inc twice. (18 sts)

Rnd 3: sc 1, inc, sc 4, [inc, sc 1] 3 times, sc 3, inc, sc 1, inc. (24 sts)

Rnds 4 and 5 (2 rnds): sc 1 in each st.

Fasten off, leaving long tail for sewing.

Using White, embroider nostrils on muzzle in straight stitch (see Techniques: Straight Stitch). Make a vertical line over Rnds 2 and 3 for each nostril, 5 sts apart. Embroider a side smile between Rnds 2 and 3, 3 sts wide.

Sew muzzle to the head centered with eyes, between Rnds 15 and 20. Stuff as you sew.

Cheeks (make 2)

Rnd 1: using Pale Pink, sc 6 in a magic ring. (6 sts)

Rnd 2: inc 6 times. (12 sts)

Fasten off invisibly, leaving long tail for sewing (see Techniques: Invisible Fasten Off).

Sew cheeks next to eyes between Rnds 16 and 19.

Horns (make 2)

Rnd 1: using Beige, sc 6 in a magic ring. (6 sts)

Rnd 2: sc 2, inc, sc 3. (7 sts)

Rnd 3: sc 3, inc, sc 3. (8 sts)

Rnd 4: sc 1 in each st.

Rnd 5: sc 3, inc, sc 4. (9 sts)

Rnd 6: sc 4, inc, sc 4. (10 sts)

Rnd 7: sc 1 in each st.

Fasten off, leaving long tail for sewing.

Stuff firmly. Sew horns on each side of head between Rnds 6 and 8, with increases on inside.

Ears (make 2)

Rnd 1: using Light Brown, sc 6 in a magic ring. (6 sts)

Rnd 2: [sc 1, inc] 3 times. (9 sts)

Rnd 3: [sc 1, inc, sc 1] 3 times. (12 sts)

Rnds 4–6 (3 rnds): sc 1 in each st.

Rnd 7: [sc 1, dec] 4 times. (8 sts)

Do not stuff. Flatten opening and work next row through both layers to close (see Techniques: Closing with Single Crochet).

Row 8: sc 4. (4 sts)

Fasten off, leaving long tail for sewing.

Flatten ears in opposite direction of last row. Sew ears below horns between Rnds 9 and 10.

Legs and body

LEG 1

Rnd 1: using Dark Brown, sc 7 in a magic ring. (7 sts)

Rnd 2: inc 7 times. (14 sts)

Rnd 3: work in BLO, sc 1 in each st.

Rnds 4 and 5 (2 rnds): sc 1 in each st.

Rnds 6–12 (7 rnds): change to Cream, sc 1 in each st.

Fasten off. Set aside.

LEG 2

Work as for leg 1, but do not fasten off at end. Cont working on body.

IF NECESSARY, ADD A FEW MORE STITCHES ON LEG 2 TO SHIFT THE COLOR CHANGE TO THE BACK OF THE LEG.

BODY

Rnd 13: still with leg 2 on hook, ch 2, sc 1 in last st of leg 1 to join (see Techniques: Joining Legs), PM here for new beg of rnd, sc 1 in each st of leg 1, inc in each ch, sc 1 in each st of leg 2, inc in each ch. (36 sts)

Rnd 14: [sc 14, inc, sc 2, inc] twice. (40 sts)

Stuff legs firmly.

Rnds 15–18 (4 rnds): sc 1 in each st.

Rnd 19: change to Sage, slst 1 in each st loosely.

Rnd 20: working in BLO of Rnd 19 and both loops of Rnd 18 (see Techniques: Straight Stripe Color Change), sc 1 in each st. (40 sts)

Rnd 21: [sc 8, dec] 4 times. (36 sts)

Rnds 22 and 23 (2 rnds): sc 1 in each st.

Rnd 24: [sc 5, dec, sc 5] 3 times. (33 sts)

Rnds 25 and 26 (2 rnds): sc 1 in each st.

8	9	10
	World Humanitarian Day	

Rnd 27: [sc 9, dec] 3 times. (30 sts)

Rnd 28: sc 1 in each st.

Rnd 29: [sc 4, dec, sc 4] 3 times. (27 sts)

Rnd 30: sc 1 in each st.

Rnd 31: [sc 7, dec] 3 times. (24 sts)

Fasten off, leaving long tail for sewing.

Stuff body firmly.

SKIRT

Using Sage, hold body with legs up and join yarn to first unworked loop of Rnd 19 with slst 1 (does not count as a st) (see Techniques: Joining Yarn to Add a Detail). Start next Rnd in same st.

Skirt is worked in closed rnds. Start each rnd with ch 2 (counts as first hdc), end each rnd with slst 1 in top of ch-2 (does not count as a st).

Rnds 1–4 (4 rnds): ch 2, hdc 39, slst 1 to ch-2 to join. (40 sts)

Rnd 5: [ch 1, slst 1] 40 times. (40 sts + 40 chs)

Fasten off and weave in yarn ends.

Sew body to bottom of head.

Arms (make 2)

Rnd 1: using Dark Brown, sc 5 in a magic ring. (5 sts)

Rnd 2: inc 5 times. (10 sts)

Rnd 3: work in BLO, sc 1 in each st. (10 sts)

Rnds 4 and 5 (2 rnds): sc 1 in each st.

Rnd 6: change to Sage, slst 1 in each st loosely.

Rnd 7: working in BLO of Rnd 6 and both loops of Rnd 5, inc in each st. (20 sts)

Rnds 8–10 (3 rnds): sc 1 in each st.

Rnd 11: [sc 2, dec] 5 times. (15 sts)

Rnds 12 and 13 (2 rnds): sc 1 in each st.

Rnd 14: [sc 1, dec] 5 times. (10 sts)

Rnd 15 and 16 (2 rnds): sc 1 in each st.

Stuff lightly. Flatten opening and work next row through both layers to close.

Row 17: sc 5. (5 sts)

Fasten off, leaving long tail for sewing.

SHIRT CUFF DETAIL

Hold arm with hand up and join Sage to first unworked loop of Rnd 6 with slst 1 (does not count as a st). Start next rnd in next st.

Rnd 1: [ch 2, slst 1] 10 times. (10 sts + 20 chs)

Fasten off invisibly and weave in yarn ends.

Sew arms on each side of body between Rnds 30 and 31.

Tail

Row 1: using Cream, ch 7, starting in 2nd ch from hook, slst 6. (6 sts)

Fasten off, leaving long tail for sewing.

Cut two 5cm (2in) strands of Light Brown. Attach to tip of tail (see Techniques: Attaching Yarn Strands). Split strands for texture. Trim to desired length.

Sew tail to back of body on Rnd 16 (see Photo 1).

Apron

Start by making front panel and strap separately.

FRONT PANEL

Row 1: using Beige, ch 11, start in 2nd ch from hook working in back bump of the ch, sc 10, turn. (10 sts)

Rows 2–6 (5 rows): ch 1, sc 1 in each st, turn. (10 sts)

Row 7: ch 2, hdc 2 in each st, turn. (20 sts)

Rows 8–10 (3 rows): ch 2, hdc 1 in each st, turn. (20 sts)

Row 11: [ch 3, skip 1 st, slst 1] 10 times. (30 sts + 10 chs)

Fasten off and weave in yarn ends.

Using Pale Pink and Sage, embroider flower details on top part of apron (see Photo 2).

NECK STRAP

Leave a long tail at the beginning of the chain for sewing later.

Row 1: using Beige, [ch 3, slst 1 in first ch] 16 times. (16 sts + 32 chs)

Fasten off, leaving long tail for sewing.

Sew one end of neck strap to one top corner of front panel. Place front panel in front of body, wrap neck strap around back of head, and sew other end to top corner of front panel.

Cut 30cm (12in) strand of Beige for waist strap. Using yarn needle, run strand up and down front panel on Row 7 (see Photo 2). Bring ends of strand to back of body and tie with a bow to secure. Tie a knot on both ends of strand to avoid splitting. Trim excess yarn.

Cut 20cm (8in) strand of Yellow to attach gold craft bell below head. Tie a bow on back to secure it. Tie a knot on both ends of strand to avoid splitting. Trim excess yarn.

Basket

Using Light Brown, work as for Cassia's basket for Rnds 1–14.

Rnd 15: slst 5, ch 6 and skip 4 sts, slst 13, ch 6 and skip 4 sts, slst 7. (33 sts)

Fasten off and weave in yarn ends.

Flowers (make 3)

Start by making blossom, leaf, and stem separately.

BLOSSOM (MAKE 1 EACH COLOR)

Rnd 1: using Pale Pink, Orange or Yellow, ch 2, start in 2nd ch from hook, sc 6 in same st. (6 sts)

Cont working in a spiral.

Rnd 2: inc in each st. (12 sts)

Rnd 3: [sc 1, inc] 6 times. (18 sts)

Rnd 4: [sc 8, inc] twice. (20 sts)

Rnds 5–10 (6 rnds): sc 1 in each st.

Fasten off invisibly, leaving long tail for shaping.

Stuff firmly leaving last two rnds unstuffed. Pull yarn tail through 5th, 10th, 15th, and 20th sts and pull tightly to shape top of flower. Weave in yarn end. Set aside.

LEAF

Rnd 1: using Yellow Green, ch 10, start in 2nd ch from hook working in back bump of ch, hdc 7, sc 1, slst 1, ch 1, cont working on other side of ch through both loops, slst 1, sc 1, hdc 6, [hdc 1, ch 1, slst 1] in same st. (19 sts)

Fasten off and weave in yarn ends. Set aside.

STEM

Rnd 1: using Yellow Green, sc 6 in a magic ring. (6 sts)

Rnds 2–5 (4 rnds): sc 1 in each st.

Leaf is attached in next rnd.

Rnd 6: sc 1 through bottom of leaf and next st of stem, sc 5. (6 sts)

Rnds 7–15 (9 rnds): sc 1 in each st.

Fasten off, leaving long tail for sewing.

Stuff stem with piece of craft chenille stem, slightly longer than stem. Insert leftover chenille stem through hole of Rnd 1 of blossom. Sew stem to bottom of blossom (see Photo 3).

SEPTEMBER

Cody Crocodile & Liam Lion

The bells are ringing, and the first class of the new school year is about to start. Liam the Lion's mom got him an adorable outfit to celebrate his first day and a new lucky pencil to take notes. Cody the Crocodile spent all summer filling out activity sheets to be prepared in case of a pop quiz, and he was the only student who brought a fresh apple for his new teacher.

CODY
10.5CM (4IN)

LIAM
11.5CM (4½IN)

PATTERN NOTES

Most pieces are worked in a spiral without joining each round. The bib of the overalls is worked in rows.

YOU WILL NEED

YARNS:

Hobbii Friends Cotton 8/4 (100% cotton) fingering (4-ply) weight, 160m (174yd) per 50g (1¾oz) ball, in the following shades:

FOR BOTH

- ✓ **Deep Pink:** 1 ball in Pink Berry Smoothie (54)
- ✓ **White:** 1 ball in White (01)

FOR CODY

- ✓ **Deep Green:** 1 ball in Emerald (105)
- ✓ **Green:** 1 ball in Parakeet (103)
- ✓ **Bright Yellow:** 1 ball in Lemon Curd (22)
- ✓ **Red:** 1 ball in Tomato (40)
- ✓ **Light Brown:** small amount in Nougat (09)

FOR LIAM

- ✓ **Mustard:** 1 ball in Mustard (28)
- ✓ **Cream:** 1 ball in Oatmilk (03)
- ✓ **Dark Orange:** 1 ball in Whisky (16)
- ✓ **Light Blue:** 1 ball in Icy Blue (76)
- ✓ **Light Gray:** small amount in Silver (118)
- ✓ **Yellow:** 1 ball in Sunflower (24)
- ✓ **Dark Gray:** 1 ball in Charcoal (123)

HOOK:

- ✓ 2.20mm (US B/1) crochet hook

TOOLS AND MATERIALS:

- ✓ 2 pairs of 6mm safety eyes
- ✓ Stitch markers
- ✓ Yarn needle
- ✓ Toy stuffing
- ✓ 1.5mm gold craft wire or ready-made doll glasses

Cody

Head

Rnd 1: using Deep Green, ch 9, start in 2nd ch from hook working in back bump of ch, inc, sc 6, sc 4 in last ch, turn, cont on other side of ch working through both loops (see Techniques: Crocheting Around Foundation Chain), sc 6, inc in last ch. (20 sts)

Rnd 2: [sc 1, inc, sc 6, inc, sc 1] twice. (24 sts)

Rnd 3: [sc 1, inc, sc 8, inc, sc 1] twice. (28 sts)

Rnd 4: sc 1 in each st.

Rnd 5: sc 3, 4-dc bobble, sc 6, 4-dc bobble (see Techniques: Bobble Stitch), sc 17. (28 sts)

Rnds 6 and 7 (2 rnds): sc 1 in each st.

Rnd 8: [sc 13, inc] twice. (30 sts)

Rnds 9 and 10 (2 rnds): sc 1 in each st.

Rnd 11: [inc, sc 6] 3 times, sc 9. (33 sts)

Rnd 12: sc 1 in each st.

Rnd 13: [inc, sc 7] 3 times, sc 9. (36 sts)

Rnds 14 and 15 (2 rnds): sc 1 in each st.

Rnd 16: [sc 1, inc] twice, sc 13, [inc, sc 1] 3 times, sc 12, inc. (42 sts)

Rnd 17: [sc 1, inc] twice, sc 17, [inc, sc 1] 3 times, sc 14, inc. (48 sts)

Rnds 18–21 (4 rnds): sc 1 in each st.

Start stuffing, cont as you work.

Rnd 22: [sc 1, dec] twice, sc 17, [dec, sc 1] 3 times, sc 14, dec. (42 sts)

Rnd 23: sc 1 in each st.

Rnd 24: [sc 6, dec, sc 6] 3 times. (39 sts)

Rnd 25: [sc 11, dec] 3 times. (36 sts)

Rnd 26: [sc 4, dec] 6 times. (30 sts)

Rnd 27: [sc 3, dec] 6 times. (24 sts)

Rnd 28: [sc 2, dec] 6 times. (18 sts)

Rnd 29: [sc 1, dec] 6 times. (12 sts)

Rnd 30: dec 6 times. (6 sts)

Fasten off, sew hole closed by pulling yarn tail through front loops of remaining sts.

Eye sockets (make 2)

Rnd 1: using Deep Green, sc 6 in a magic ring. (6 sts)

Rnd 2: inc 6 times. (12 sts)

Rnd 3: [sc 3, inc] 3 times. (15 sts)

Rnds 4 and 5 (2 rnds): sc 1 in each st.

Fasten off, leaving long tail for sewing.

Place a safety eye between Rnds 4 and 5 of each eye socket (see Photo 1). Stuff remaining space firmly.

Sew eye sockets to top of head between Rnds 17 and 21, 4 sts apart (see Photo 1).

Cheeks (make 2)

Rnd 1: using Deep Pink, sc 6 in a magic ring. (6 sts)

Rnd 2: inc 6 times. (12 sts)

Fasten off invisibly, leaving long tail for sewing (see Techniques: Invisible Fasten Off).

Sew cheeks on each side of head between Rnds 18 and 20, 2 sts below eye sockets (see Photo 2).

Embroider face details using straight stitch (see Techniques: Straight Stitch). Using Green make four horizontal lines between nostrils and eye sockets (see Photo 3).

Using White, embroider mouth across head using straight stitches. Use sewing pins to plan direction of mouth. Make short lines from Rnd 14 on one side of head to other, adding crooked lines for teeth (see Photos 1 and 2).

Body

Rnd 1: using Deep Green, sc 6 in a magic ring. (6 sts)

Rnd 2: inc 6 times. (12 sts)

Rnd 3: [sc 1, inc] 6 times. (18 sts)

Rnd 4: [sc 2, inc] 6 times. (24 sts)

Rnd 5: [sc 3, inc] 6 times. (30 sts)

Rnd 6: [sc 4, inc] 6 times. (36 sts)

8 International Literacy Day	9	10

Rnd 7: [sc 5, inc] 6 times. (42 sts)

Rnd 8: [sc 6, inc] 6 times. (48 sts)

Rnds 9–11 (3 rnds): sc 1 in each st.

Rnd 12: change to Bright Yellow, slst 1 in each st loosely.

Rnd 13: working in BLO of Rnd 12 and both loops of Rnd 11 (see Techniques: Straight Stripe Color Change), sc 1 in each st. (48 sts)

Rnd 14: [sc 5, dec, sc 5] 4 times. (44 sts)

Rnd 15: sc 1 in each st.

Rnd 16: [sc 9, dec] 4 times. (40 sts)

Rnd 17: sc 1 in each st.

Rnd 18: [sc 4, dec, sc 4] 4 times. (36 sts)

Rnd 19: sc 1 in each st.

Rnd 20: [sc 7, dec] 4 times. (32 sts)

Rnd 21: sc 1 in each st.

Rnd 22: [sc 3, dec, sc 3] 4 times. (28 sts)

Rnd 23: [sc 5, dec] 4 times, turn. (24 sts)

Cont working in opposite direction.

Rnd 24: change to White, ch 1, working in BLO, hdc 8, dc 3, ch 3, slst 1, ch 3, dc 3, hdc 9, slst 1 to first st to join. (24 sts)

Fasten off, leaving long tail for sewing.

Stuff firmly.

SHIRT HEM DETAIL

Hold body upside down and join Bright Yellow to first unworked loop of Rnd 12 with slst 1 (counts as first stitch of next rnd).

Rnd 1: slst 1 in each st. (48 sts)

Fasten off invisibly and weave in yarn ends.

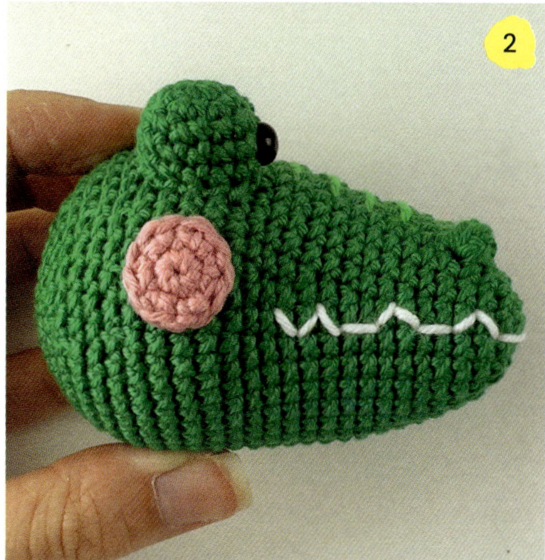

Sew body to bottom of head between Rnds 15 and 22, using unworked loops of Rnd 23. Slst from Rnd 24 should be aligned with face.

Legs (make 2)

Rnd 1: using Deep Green, ch 5, start in 2nd ch from hook working in back bump of ch, inc, sc 2, sc 4 in last ch, turn, cont on other side of ch working through both loops, sc 2, inc in last ch. (12 sts)

Rnd 2: sc 1, inc, sc 2, inc 4 times, sc 2, inc, sc 1. (18 sts)

Rnd 3: sc 1 in each st.

Rnd 4: sc 7, [4-dc bobble, sc 1] 3 times, sc 5. (18 sts)

Rnd 5: sc 1 in each st.

Rnd 6: sc 7, dec 3 times, sc 5. (15 sts)

Rnd 7: sc 5, dec 3 times, sc 4. (12 sts)

Stuff firmly to here.

Rnds 8–11 (4 rnds): sc 1 in each st.

IF NECESSARY, ADD OR UNDO A FEW STITCHES TO REACH THE BOTTOM OF THE LEG.

Stuff rest of leg lightly. Flatten opening and work next row through both layers to close (see Techniques: Closing with Single Crochet).

Row 12: sc 6. (6 sts)

Fasten off, leaving long tail for sewing.

Sew legs on each side of body between Rnds 6 and 11. Secure middle of the legs to the body with a few sewn stitches. Cody the Crocodile should be able to sit on a flat surface.

Arms (make 2)

Rnd 1: using Deep Green, sc 5 in a magic ring. (5 sts)

Rnd 2: inc 5 times. (10 sts)

Rnds 3–8 (6 rnds): sc 1 in each st.

Rnd 9: change to Bright Yellow, slst 1 in each st loosely. (10 sts)

Rnd 10: working in BLO of Rnd 9 and both loops of Rnd 8, sc 1 in each st. (10 sts)

Rnds 11 and 12 (2 rnds): sc 1 in each st.

Stuff lightly. Flatten opening and work next row through both layers to close.

Row 13: sc 5. (5 sts)

Fasten off, leaving long tail for sewing.

SHIRT CUFF DETAIL

Hold arm with hand up and join Bright Yellow to first unworked loop of Rnd 9 with slst 1 (counts as first st of next rnd).

Rnd 1: slst 1 in each st. (10 sts)

Fasten off invisibly and weave in yarn ends.

Sew arms on each side of body, slightly pointing forward, between Rnds 18 and 22. Secure middle of arms to the body with a few sewn stitches.

Tail

Rnd 1: using Deep Green, sc 6 in a magic ring. (6 sts)

Rnd 2: [sc 1, inc] 3 times. (9 sts)

Rnd 3: sc 1 in each st.

Rnd 4: [sc 2, inc] 3 times. (12 sts)

Rnds 5 and 6 (2 rnds): sc 1 in each st.

Rnd 7: [sc 3, inc] 3 times. (15 sts)

Rnd 8: sc 1 in each st.

Rnd 9: [sc 4, inc] 3 times. (18 sts)

Rnds 10 and 11 (2 rnds): sc 1 in each st.

Rnd 12: [sc 5, inc] 3 times. (21 sts)

Rnds 13 and 14 (2 rnds): sc 1 in each st.

Fasten off, leaving long tail for sewing.

Stuff tail firmly.

Using Green, embroider spikes across tail.

Sew tail to back of body between Rnds 6 and 11 (see Photo 4).

Apple

Start by making fruit, stem, and leaf separately.

FRUIT

Rnd 1: using Red, sc 6 in a magic ring. (6 sts)

Rnd 2: working in FLO, inc 6 times. (12 sts)

Rnd 3: [sc 1, inc] 6 times. (18 sts)

Rnd 4: [sc 2, inc] 6 times. (24 sts)

Rnds 5–9 (5 rnds): sc 1 in each st.

Rnd 10: [sc 3, dec, sc 3] 3 times. (21 sts)

Rnd 11: [sc 5, dec] 3 times. (18 sts)

Rnd 12: [sc 1, dec] 6 times. (12 sts)

Stuff firmly.

Rnd 13: dec 6 times. (6 sts)

Fasten off, leaving long tail for shaping, and sew hole closed by pulling yarn tail through front loops of remaining sts.

Using yarn needle, run yarn tail inside apple and exit through magic ring. Insert yarn needle through a stitch of Rnd 1 and exit at bottom. Pull tightly to shape (see Photo 5). Hide yarn tail inside apple.

STEM

Row 1: using Light Brown, ch 5, start in 2nd ch from hook working in back bump of ch, slst 4. (4 sts)

Fasten off, leaving long tail for sewing.

Sew stem to top of fruit.

LEAF

Rnd 1: using Green, ch 6, start in 3rd ch from hook working in back bump of ch, hdc 2, sc 1, slst 1, ch 1, cont on other side of ch working through both loops, slst 1, sc 1, hdc 1, [hdc 1, ch 2, slst 1] in last ch. (9 sts)

Fasten off, leaving long tail for sewing.

Sew leaf to top of apple next to stem.

Glasses

Using gold craft wire, create glasses (see Techniques: Making Doll Glasses) or use ready-made doll glasses. Attach glasses to top of head between eyes with craft glue or a few sewn stitches using White to resemble tape on broken glasses (see Photo 6).

4

5

6

Liam

Head

Rnd 1: using Mustard, sc 6 in a magic ring. (6 sts)

Rnd 2: inc 6 times. (12 sts)

Rnd 3: [sc 1, inc] 6 times. (18 sts)

Rnd 4: [sc 2, inc] 6 times. (24 sts)

Rnd 5: [sc 3, inc] 6 times. (30 sts)

Rnd 6: [sc 4, inc] 6 times. (36 sts)

Rnd 7: [sc 5, inc] 6 times. (42 sts)

Rnd 8: [sc 6, inc] 6 times. (48 sts)

Rnd 9: [sc 15, inc] 3 times. (51 sts)

Rnd 10: [sc 8, inc, sc 8] 3 times. (54 sts)

Rnds 11–19 (9 rnds): sc 1 in each st.

Rnd 20: [sc 7, dec] 6 times. (48 sts)

Rnd 21: [sc 6, dec] 6 times. (42 sts)

Rnd 22: [sc 5, dec] 6 times. (36 sts)

Place safety eyes between Rnds 15 and 16, 10 sts apart.

Start stuffing, cont as you work.

Rnd 23: [sc 4, dec] 6 times. (30 sts)

Rnd 24: [sc 3, dec] 6 times. (24 sts)

Rnd 25: [sc 2, dec] 6 times. (18 sts)

Rnd 26: [sc 1, dec] 6 times. (12 sts)

Rnd 27: dec 6 times. (6 sts)

Fasten off, sew hole closed by pulling yarn tail through front loops of remaining sts.

Muzzle

Rnd 1: using Cream, sc 6 in a magic ring. (6 sts)

Rnd 2: inc 6 times. (12 sts)

Rnd 3: [sc 1, inc] 6 times. (18 sts)

Rnds 4 and 5 (2 rnds): sc 1 in each st.

Fasten off, leaving long tail for sewing.

Using Dark Gray, embroider nose on muzzle using straight stitch (see Techniques: Straight Stitch). Make four horizontal lines between Rnds 2 and 3, 4 sts wide. Make a vertical line centered with nose, 2 rnds tall, and a smile at bottom between Rnds 2 and 3 (see Photo 1).

Sew muzzle to the head centered with eyes, between Rnds 14 and 19. Stuff as you sew (see Photo 1).

Cheeks (make 2)

Rnd 1: using Deep Pink, sc 6 in a magic ring. (6 sts)

Rnd 2: inc 6 times. (12 sts)

Fasten off invisibly, leaving long tail for sewing (see Techniques: Invisible Fasten Off).

Sew cheeks next to eyes between Rnds 16 and 19 (see Photo 1).

Ears (make 2)

Rnd 1: using Mustard, sc 6 in a magic ring. (6 sts)

Rnd 2: inc 6 times. (12 sts)

Rnds 3 and 4 (2 rnds): sc 1 in each st.

Fasten off, leaving long tail for sewing.

Do not stuff. Flatten ears into a semi-circle.

Sew ears to head between Rnds 6 and 10, 6 sts away from eyes (see Photo 1).

Body

Rnd 1: using Deep Pink, sc 6 in a magic ring. (6 sts)

Rnd 2: inc 6 times. (12 sts)

Rnd 3: [sc 1, inc] 6 times. (18 sts)

Rnd 4: [sc 2, inc] 6 times. (24 sts)

Rnd 5: [sc 3, inc] 6 times. (30 sts)

Rnd 6: [sc 4, inc] 6 times. (36 sts)

Rnd 7: [sc 5, inc] 6 times. (42 sts)

Rnd 8: [sc 6, inc] 6 times. (48 sts)

Rnds 9–11 (3 rnds): sc 1 in each st.

Rnd 12: change to Light Blue, working in BLO, sc 1 in each st.

Rnd 13: [sc 5, dec, sc 5] 4 times. (44 sts)

Rnd 14: change to White, sc 1 in each st.

Rnd 15: change to Light Blue, [sc 9, dec] 4 times. (40 sts)

Rnd 16: sc 1 in each st.

Rnd 17: change to White, [sc 4, dec, sc 4] 4 times. (36 sts)

Rnd 18: change to Light Blue, sc 1 in each st.

Rnd 19: [sc 7, dec] 4 times. (32 sts)

Rnd 20: change to White, sc 1 in each st.

Rnd 21: change to Light Blue, [sc 3, dec, sc 3] 4 times. (28 sts)

Rnd 22: [sc 5, dec] 4 times. (24 sts)

Fasten off, leaving long tail for sewing.

Stuff firmly.

OVERALL BIB

Hold body up and join Deep Pink to 21st unworked loop of Rnd 11 with slst 1 (does not count as a st) (see Techniques: Joining Yarn to Add a Detail). Start next row in same st.

Row 1: ch 1, sc 8, turn. (8 sts)

Rows 2–4 (3 rows): ch 1, sc 8, turn.

Row 5: ch 1, sc 8. (8 sts)

Cont working around overall bib and remaining unworked loops of Rnd 11 of body.

Rnd 6: ch 1, work on side of rows, sc 5, work on Rnd 11, sc 40, work on side of rows, sc 5, ch 1, work on Row 5, sc 8 (see Photo 2). (58 sts)

Fasten off invisibly and weave in yarn ends.

Sew body to bottom of head with overall bib aligned with face.

Mane

Row 1: using Dark Orange, ch 52, starting in 3rd ch from hook, dc 3 in each ch. (150 sts)

Fasten off, leaving long tail for sewing.

Place mane around head behind ears and cheeks. Join ends of mane by adding a few sewn stitches with yarn tail. Sew mane in place (see Photo 3).

1

2

3

Legs (make 2)

Rnd 1: using Mustard, sc 6 in a magic ring. (6 sts)

Rnd 2: inc 6 times. (12 sts)

Rnd 3: [sc 1, inc] 6 times. (18 sts)

Rnds 4–6 (3 rnds): sc 1 in each st.

Rnd 7: sc 4, dec 5 times, sc 4. (13 sts)

Rnd 8: sc 5, sc3tog, sc 5. (11 sts)

Stuff firmly to here.

Rnds 9–11 (3 rnds): sc 1 in each st.

IF NECESSARY, ADD OR UNDO A FEW STITCHES TO REACH THE BOTTOM OF THE LEG.

Stuff rest of leg lightly. Flatten opening and work next row through both layers to close (see Techniques: Closing with Single Crochet).

Row 12: sc 5, leave 1 st unworked. (5 sts)

Fasten off, leaving long tail for sewing.

Sew legs on each side of body between Rnds 6 and 10. Secure middle of legs to body with a few sewn stitches. Liam the Lion should be able to sit on a flat surface.

Arms (make 2)

Rnd 1: using Mustard, sc 5 in a magic ring. (5 sts)

Rnd 2: inc 5 times. (10 sts)

Rnds 3–8 (6 rnds): sc 1 in each st.

Rnd 9: change to Light Blue, slst 1 in each st loosely.

Rnd 10: working in BLO of Rnd 9 and both loops of Rnd 8 (see Techniques: Straight Stripe Color Change), sc 1 in each st. (10 sts)

Rnd 11: change to White, sc 1 in each st.

Rnd 12: change to Light Blue, sc 1 in each st.

Stuff lightly. Flatten opening and work next row through both layers to close.

Row 13: sc 5. (5 sts)

Fasten off, leaving long tail for sewing.

SHIRT CUFF DETAIL

Hold arm with hand up and join Light Blue to first unworked loop of Rnd 9 with slst 1 (counts as first stitch of next rnd).

Rnd 1: slst 1 in each st. (10 sts)

Fasten off invisibly and weave in yarn ends.

Sew arms on each side of body, slightly pointing forward, between Rnds 17 and 21. Secure middle of arms to body with a few sewn stitches.

Straps (make 2)

Row 1: using Deep Pink, ch 25, start in 2nd ch from hook working in the back bump of the ch, slst 24. (24 sts)

Fasten off, leaving long tail for sewing.

Sew straps to top corners of overall bib, and on Rnd 11 on back of body, with straps crossed (see Photo 4).

Using Light Blue, embroider French knots (see Techniques: French Knot) where straps are sewn at front.

Tail

Rnd 1: using Dark Orange, sc 6 in a magic ring. (6 sts)

Rnd 2: [sc 1, inc] 3 times. (9 sts)

Rnd 3: sc 1 in each st.

Rnd 4: [sc 2, inc] 3 times. (12 sts)

Rnds 5 and 6 (2 rnds): sc 1 in each st.

Stuff firmly to here.

Rnd 7: dec 6 times. (6 sts)

Rnds 8–17 (10 rnds): change to Mustard, sc 1 in each st.

Fasten off, leaving long tail for sewing.

Sew tail to back of the body on Rnd 7 (see Photo 5).

Pencil

Rnd 1: using Deep Pink, sc 5 in a magic ring. (5 sts)

Rnd 2: inc 5 times. (10 sts)

Rnd 3: [sc 1, inc] 3 times. (15 sts)

Rnd 4: work in BLO, sc 1 in each st.

Rnds 5 and 6 (2 rnds): sc 1 in each st.

Rnd 7: change to Light Gray, sc 1 in each st.

Start stuffing, cont as you work.

Rnds 8–19 (12 rnds): change to Yellow, sc 1 in each st.

Rnd 20: change to Cream, sc 1 in each st.

Rnd 21: [sc 3, dec] 3 times. (12 sts)

Rnd 22: sc 1 in each st.

Rnd 23: [sc 2, dec] 3 times. (9 sts)

Rnd 24: sc 1 in each st.

Rnd 25: change to Dark Gray, [sc 1, dec] 3 times. (6 sts)

Rnd 26: dec 3 times. (3 sts)

Fasten off, sew hole closed by pulling yarn tail through front loops of remaining sts (see Photo 6).

5

6

Rusty Raven & Olivia Owl

It's close to midnight on Halloween, and all the scary beings are ready to party on this special occasion. Rusty the Raven and Olivia the Owl are known to throw the best costume parties in all the realm, so be sure to practice your dance steps, and don't get scared if you see a few skulls and jack-o'-lanterns come to life!

RUSTY 17CM (6¾IN)   OLIVIA 17CM (6¾IN)

PATTERN NOTES

Most pieces are worked in a spiral without joining each round. The tail, straps, collars, and jack-o'-lantern stem are worked in rows. The eye patches are worked in closed rounds.

DIFFICULTY LEVEL ☒☒☒

YOU WILL NEED

YARNS:

Hobbii Friends Cotton 8/4 (100% cotton) fingering (4-ply) weight, 160m (174yd) per 50g (1¾oz) ball, in the following shades:

FOR BOTH

- ✓ **Dark Gray:** 1 ball in Charcoal (123)
- ✓ **White:** 1 ball in White (01)
- ✓ **Dark Orange:** 1 ball in Whisky (16)

FOR RUSTY

- ✓ **Light Gray:** 1 ball in Silver (118)

FOR OLIVIA

- ✓ **Dark Yellow:** 1 ball in Dark Yellow (26)

HOOK:

- ✓ 2.20mm (US B/1) crochet hook

TOOLS AND MATERIALS:

- ✓ 1 pair of 8mm safety eyes
- ✓ 1 pair of 10mm safety eyes
- ✓ Stitch markers
- ✓ Yarn needle
- ✓ Toy stuffing
- ✓ Small pompom maker
- ✓ 2 small white buttons
- ✓ Sewing needle and dark gray thread

Rusty

Head

Rnd 1: using Dark Gray, sc 6 in a magic ring. (6 sts)

Rnd 2: inc 6 times. (12 sts)

Rnd 3: [sc 1, inc] 6 times. (18 sts)

Rnd 4: [sc 2, inc] 6 times. (24 sts)

Rnd 5: [sc 3, inc] 6 times. (30 sts)

Rnd 6: [sc 4, inc] 6 times. (36 sts)

Rnd 7: [sc 5, inc] 6 times. (42 sts)

Rnd 8: [sc 6, inc] 6 times. (48 sts)

Rnds 9–13 (5 rnds): sc 1 in each st.

Rnd 14: [sc 7, inc] 6 times. (54 sts)

Rnds 15–19 (5 rnds): sc 1 in each st.

Rnd 20: [sc 7, dec] 6 times. (48 sts)

Rnd 21: [sc 6, dec] 6 times. (42 sts)

Rnd 22: [sc 5, dec] 6 times. (36 sts)

Place 8mm safety eyes between Rnds 14 and 15, 10 sts apart (see Photo 1).

Start stuffing, cont as you work.

Rnd 23: [sc 4, dec] 6 times. (30 sts)

Rnd 24: [sc 3, dec] 6 times. (24 sts)

Rnd 25: [sc 2, dec] 6 times. (18 sts)

Rnd 26: [sc 1, dec] 6 times. (12 sts)

Rnd 27: dec 6 times. (6 sts)

Fasten off, sew hole closed by pulling yarn tail through front loops of remaining sts.

Using White and straight stitch (see Techniques: Straight Stitch), embroider two lines on outer side of each eye for depth (see Photo 1).

Cheeks (make 2)

Rnd 1: using Dark Orange, sc 6 in a magic ring. (6 sts)

Rnd 2: inc 6 times. (12 sts)

Fasten off invisibly, leaving long tail for sewing (see Techniques: Invisible Fasten Off).

Sew cheeks next to eyes between Rnds 15 and 18 (see Photo 2).

Beak

Rnd 1: using Light Gray, sc 6 in a magic ring. (6 sts)

Rnd 2: sc 2, inc twice, sc 2. (8 sts)

Rnd 3: sc 3, inc twice, sc 3. (10 sts)

Rnd 4: sc 4, inc twice, sc 4. (12 sts)

Rnds 5 and 6 (2 rnds): sc 1 in each st.

Fasten off, leaving long tail for sewing.

Stuff beak firmly.

Sew beak to the head centered with eyes between Rnds 14 and 17, with the increases at the top (see Photo 2).

Body

Rnd 1: using Dark Orange, sc 6 in a magic ring. (6 sts)

Rnd 2: inc 6 times. (12 sts)

Rnd 3: [sc 1, inc] 6 times. (18 sts)

Rnd 4: [sc 2, inc] 6 times. (24 sts)

Rnd 5: [sc 3, inc] 6 times. (30 sts)

Rnd 6: [sc 4, inc] 6 times. (36 sts)

Rnd 7: [sc 5, inc] 6 times. (42 sts)

Rnd 8: [sc 6, inc] 6 times. (48 sts)

Cont alternating from Dark Orange to White to make diamond pattern.

Rnd 9: [(Dark Orange) sc 3, (White) sc 1, (Dark Orange) sc 2] 8 times. (48 sts)

Rnd 10: [(Dark Orange) sc 2, (White) sc 3, (Dark Orange) sc 1] 8 times. (48 sts)

Rnd 11: [(Dark Orange) sc 1, (White) sc 5] 8 times. (48 sts)

Rnd 12: [(Dark Orange) sc 2, (White) sc 3, (Dark Orange) sc 1] 8 times. (48 sts)

Rnd 13: [(Dark Orange) sc 3, (White) sc 1, (Dark Orange) sc 2] 8 times. (48 sts)

Cont working in Dark Orange only.

Rnd 14: [sc 7, dec, sc 7] 3 times. (45 sts)

Rnd 15: change to Dark Gray, working in BLO, sc 1 in each st.

Rnd 16: [sc 13, dec] 3 times. (42 sts)

Rnd 17: sc 1 in each st.

Rnd 18: [sc 6, dec, sc 6] 3 times. (39 sts)

Rnd 19: sc 1 in each st.

Rnd 20: [sc 11, dec] 3 times. (36 sts)

Rnd 21: sc 1 in each st.

Rnd 22: [sc 5, dec, sc 5] 3 times. (33 sts)

Rnd 23: [sc 9, dec] 3 times. (30 sts)

Rnd 24: [sc 3, dec] 6 times. (24 sts)

Fasten off, leaving long tail for sewing.

Stuff body firmly.

SHORTS WAISTBAND DETAIL

Hold body upside down and attach Dark Orange with slst 1 (does not count as a st) to first unworked loop of Rnd 14 (see Techniques: Joining Yarn to Add a Detail). Start next rnd in same st.

Rnd 1: slst 1 in each st. (45 sts)

Fasten off and weave in yarn ends.

Sew body to bottom of head.

Feet (make 2)

Start by making toes.

TOES (MAKE 2 FOR EACH FOOT)

Rnd 1: using Light Gray, sc 6 in a magic ring. (6 sts)

Rnds 2 and 3 (2 rnds): sc 1 in each st.

Fasten off first toe. Do not fasten off 2nd toe.

Do not stuff.

JOINING THE TOES

Rnd 4: still with 2nd toe on hook, sc 1 in last st of first toe to join, PM here for new beg of rnd, sc 1 in each st of first toe, sc 1 in each st of 2nd toe. (12 sts)

Rnd 5: [sc 2, dec] 3 times. (9 sts)

Rnd 6: [sc 1, dec] 3 times. (6 sts)

Rnd 7: sc 1 in each st.

Fasten off, leaving long tail for sewing, and sew hole closed by pulling yarn tail through front loops of remaining sts.

Bring yarn tail to top of Y-shaped foot (see Photo 3).

29	30	31 Halloween

Legs (make 2)

Rnd 1: using Light Gray, sc 6 in a magic ring. (6 sts)

Rnds 2 and 3 (2 rnds): sc 1 in each st.

Rnd 4: change to Dark Gray, inc 6 times. (12 sts)

Rnds 5 and 6 (2 rnds): sc 1 in each st.

Fasten off, leaving long tail for sewing.

Stuff firmly.

Sew center of feet to legs. Sew legs to front of body between Rnds 8 and 11, 7 sts apart. Rusty the Raven should be able to sit on a flat surface.

Wings (make 2)

Rnd 1: using Dark Gray, sc 6 in a magic ring. (6 sts)

Rnd 2: inc 6 times. (12 sts)

Rnd 3: [sc 3, inc] 3 times. (15 sts)

Rnd 4: [sc 2, inc, sc 2] 3 times. (18 sts)

Rnds 5–8 (4 rnds): sc 1 in each st.

Rnd 9: [sc 2, dec, sc 2] 3 times. (15 sts)

Rnd 10: [sc 3, dec] 3 times. (12 sts)

Do not stuff. Flatten opening and work next row through both layers to close (see Techniques: Closing with Single Crochet).

Row 11: [ch 3, start in 2nd ch from hook, slst 2 on ch, slst 1 in next st] 6 times. (6 feathers + 6 sts)

Fasten off, leaving long tail for sewing.

Bring yarn tail through magic ring of wing. Sew wings on each side of body between Rnds 21 and 22. Sew only portion of wings between sewing pins as shown (see Photo 4).

Tail

Row 1: using Dark Gray, [ch 7, start in 3rd ch from hook working in back bump of ch, hdc 3, sc 2] 3 times. (3 feathers)

Fasten off, leaving long tail for sewing.

Sew tail to the back of body on Rnd 8 (see Photo 5).

Straps (make 2)

Row 1: using White, ch 31, start in 2nd ch from hook working in back bump of ch, sc 24, end row here. (24 sts)

Row 2: ch 25, start in 2nd ch from hook working in back bump of ch, sc 24, working in back bump of remaining ch from Row 1, sc 6. (30 sts)

Fasten off, leaving long tail for sewing.

Sew bottom of Y-shaped straps to back of body on shorts waistband detail (see Photo 6). Sew other two extremities to front of body also on shorts waistband detail, 13 sts apart.

Using Dark Orange, embroider a French knot (see Embroidery: French Knot) on strap at front where they overlap waistband.

Hat

Rnd 1: using White, sc 6 in a magic ring. (6 sts)

Rnd 2: [sc 1, inc] 3 times. (9 sts)

Rnd 3: change to Dark Gray, sc 1 in each st.

Rnd 4: [sc 1, inc, sc 1] 3 times. (12 sts)

Rnd 5: change to White, sc 1 in each st.

Rnd 6: [sc 3, inc] 3 times. (15 sts)

Rnd 7: change to Dark Gray, sc 1 in each st.

Rnd 8: [sc 2, inc, sc 2] 3 times. (18 sts)

Rnd 9: change to White, sc 1 in each st.

Rnd 10: [sc 5, inc] 3 times. (21 sts)

Rnd 11: change to Dark Gray, sc 1 in each st.

Rnd 12: [sc 3, inc, sc 3] 3 times. (24 sts)

Rnd 13: change to Dark Orange, working in FLO, [hdc 1, ch 2, hdc 1] in same st 24 times. (48 sts + 48 chs)

Fasten off, leaving long tail for sewing.

Using Dark Orange, make a small pompom and attach to top of hat.

Stuff hat firmly. Sew hat to top of head using unworked loops from Rnd 12.

Collars (make 1 in each color)

LEAVE A LONG TAIL AT THE BEGINNING OF THE CHAIN FOR ATTACHING LATER.

Row 1: using Dark Orange / White, ch 29, start in 3rd ch from hook working in back bump of ch, hdc 2 in each ch, turn. (54 sts)

Row 2: ch 2, hdc 54. (54 sts)

Fasten off, leaving long tail for attaching.

Using yarn needle, weave yarn tail to end of beginning ch. Place collars below head and tie a knot with a bow with yarn tails to secure them. Tie a knot on ends of strands to avoid splitting. Trim excess yarn.

Skull

Rnd 1: using White, sc 6 in a magic ring. (6 sts)

Rnd 2: inc 6 times. (12 sts)

Rnd 3: [sc 1, inc] 6 times. (18 sts)

Rnd 4: [sc 2, inc] 6 times. (24 sts)

Rnds 5–9 (5 rnds): sc 1 in each st.

Rnd 10: dec 6 times, sc 12. (18 sts)

Rnd 11: sc3tog twice, sc 12. (14 sts)

Stuff firmly.

Rnd 12: working in BLO, dec 7 times. (7 sts)

Fasten off, sew hole closed by pulling yarn tail through front loops of remaining sts.

Using Dark Gray, embroider face on skull using straight stitch. Make three vertical lines for each eye over Rnds 7 and 8, 4 sts apart. Make an inverted "V" between eyes on Rnd 9 for nose. Make five vertical lines on Rnd 11 for teeth.

4

5

6

Olivia

Eye patches (make 2)

The eye patches are worked in closed rnds starting with a magic ring. Start each rnd with ch 1 (does not count as a st), and end with slst 1 on first st (does not count as a st).

Rnd 1: using Dark Yellow, ch 1, sc 6 in a magic ring, slst 1 to first st to join. (6 sts)

DO NOT COMPLETELY CLOSE THE MAGIC RING TO LEAVE SPACE TO PLACE THE SAFETY EYES.

Rnd 2: ch 1, inc 6 times, slst 1 to first st to join. (12 sts)

Rnd 3: ch 1, [sc 1, inc] 6 times, slst 1 to first st to join. (18 sts)

Rnd 4: change to Dark Orange, ch 1, inc, sc 2, hdc 2 in same st, hdc 2, [dc 2 in same st, dc 2] twice, dc 2 in same st, hdc 2, hdc 2 in same st, sc 2, slst 1 to first st to join. (24 sts)

Fasten off, leaving long tail for sewing.

Head

Rnd 1: using Dark Gray, sc 6 in a magic ring. (6 sts)

Rnd 2: inc 6 times. (12 sts)

Rnd 3: [sc 1, inc] 6 times. (18 sts)

Rnd 4: [sc 2, inc] 6 times. (24 sts)

Rnd 5: [sc 3, inc] 6 times. (30 sts)

Rnd 6: [sc 4, inc] 6 times. (36 sts)

Rnd 7: [sc 5, inc] 6 times. (42 sts)

Rnd 8: [sc 6, inc] 6 times. (48 sts)

Rnds 9–11 (3 rnds): sc 1 in each st.

Rnd 12: [sc 15, inc] 3 times. (51 sts)

Rnd 13: [sc 8, inc, sc 8] 3 times. (54 sts)

Rnds 14–19 (6 rnds): sc 1 in each st.

Rnd 20: [sc 7, dec] 6 times. (48 sts)

Rnd 21: [sc 6, dec] 6 times. (42 sts)

Rnd 22: [sc 5, dec] 6 times. (36 sts)

Place 10mm safety eyes through magic ring of eye patches, then insert safety eyes on head between Rnds 14 and 15, 10 sts apart. First inc of eye patches should be facing center. Secure safety eyes inside head.

Sew eye patches to head now or after stuffing.

Start stuffing, cont as you work.

Rnd 23: [sc 4, dec] 6 times. (30 sts)

Rnd 24: [sc 3, dec] 6 times. (24 sts)

Rnd 25: [sc 2, dec] 6 times. (18 sts)

Rnd 26: [sc 1, dec] 6 times. (12 sts)

Rnd 27: dec 6 times. (6 sts)

Fasten off, sew hole closed by pulling yarn tail through front loops of remaining sts.

Using Dark Orange, embroider the head markings in straight stitch (see Techniques: Straight Stitch). Make three double lines centered with eye patches between Rnds 7 and 10.

Beak

Rnd 1: using Dark Yellow, sc 6 in a magic ring. (6 sts)

Rnd 2: [sc 2, inc] twice. (8 sts)

Rnds 3 and 4 (2 rnds): sc 1 in each st.

Rnd 5: [sc 2, dec] twice. (6 sts)

Do not stuff.

Fasten off, leaving long tail for sewing, sew hole closed by pulling yarn tail through front loops of remaining sts.

Sew beak to the head centered with eye patches between Rnds 14 and 17.

Ears (make 2)

Rnd 1: using Dark Gray, sc 6 in a magic ring. (6 sts)

Rnd 2: [sc 1, inc] 3 times. (9 sts)

Rnds 3 and 4 (2 rnds): sc 1 in each st.

Fasten off, leaving long tail for sewing.

Do not stuff.

Cut cut four 5cm (2in) strands of Dark Gray. Attach two to tip of each ear (see Techniques: Attaching Yarn Strands). Split strands for texture. Trim to desired length.

Sew ears to top of head between Rnds 6 and 9.

Body

Rnd 1: using Dark Orange, sc 6 in a magic ring. (6 sts)

Cont alternating from Dark Orange to White to make stripes.

Rnd 2: [(Dark Orange) inc, (White) inc] 3 times. (12 sts)

Rnd 3: [(Dark Orange) sc 1, inc, (White) sc 1, inc] 3 times. (18 sts)

Rnd 4: [(Dark Orange) sc 1, inc, sc 1, (White) sc 1, inc, sc 1] 3 times. (24 sts)

Rnd 5: [(Dark Orange) sc 3, inc, (White) sc 3, inc] 3 times. (30 sts)

Rnd 6: [(Dark Orange) sc 2, inc, sc 2, (White) sc 2, inc, sc 2] 3 times. (36 sts)

Rnd 7: [(Dark Orange) sc 5, inc, (White) sc 5, inc] 3 times. (42 sts)

Rnd 8: [(Dark Orange) sc 3, inc, sc 3, (White) sc 3, inc, sc 3] 3 times. (48 sts)

Rnds 9–13 (5 rnds): [(Dark Orange) sc 8, (White) sc 8] 3 times. (48 sts)

Rnd 14: [(Dark Orange) sc 8, (White) sc 3, dec, sc 3] 3 times. (45 sts)

Rnd 15: [(Dark Orange) sc 8, (White) sc 7] 3 times. (45 sts)

Rnd 16: [(Dark Orange) sc 3, dec, sc 3, (White) sc 7] 3 times. (42 sts)

Rnd 17: [(Dark Orange) sc 7, (White) sc 7] 3 times. (42 sts)

Rnd 18: [(Dark Orange) sc 7, (White) sc 3, dec, sc 2] 3 times. (39 sts)

Rnd 19: [(Dark Orange) sc 7, (White) sc 6] 3 times. (39 sts)

Rnd 20: [(Dark Orange) sc 3, dec, sc 2, (White) sc 6] 3 times. (36 sts)

Rnd 21: [(Dark Orange) sc 6, (White) sc 6] 3 times. (36 sts)

Rnd 22: [(Dark Orange) sc 6, (White) sc 2, dec, sc 2] 3 times. (33 sts)

Rnd 23: [(Dark Orange) sc 2, dec, sc 2, (White) sc 5] 3 times. (30 sts)

Rnd 24: [(Dark Orange) sc 2, dec, sc 1, (White) sc 2, dec, sc 1] 3 times, turn. (24 sts)

Cont working in opposite direction.

Rnd 25: change to Yellow, working in BLO, [hdc 1, dc 2 in same st, hdc 1, slst 1] 6 times. (30 sts)

Fasten off, leaving long tail for sewing.

Stuff body firmly.

Sew body to bottom of head using unworked loops of Rnd 24. One Dark Orange vertical stripe should be centered with face.

Sew buttons to front of body, on stripe centered with face. First button is between Rnds 13 and 14, 2nd is between Rnds 19 and 20.

Feet (make 2)

Start by making toes.

TOES (MAKE 2 FOR EACH FOOT)

Rnd 1: using Dark Yellow, sc 6 in a magic ring. (6 sts)

Rnds 2 and 3 (2 rnds): sc 1 in each st.

Fasten off first toe. Do not fasten off 2nd toe.

Do not stuff.

JOINING THE TOES

Rnd 4: still with 2nd toe on hook, sc 1 in last st of first toe to join, PM here for new beg of rnd, sc 1 in each st of first toe, sc 1 in each st of 2nd toe. (12 sts)

Rnd 5: [sc 2, dec] 3 times. (9 sts)

Rnd 6: [sc 1, dec] 3 times. (6 sts)

Rnd 7: sc 1 in each st.

Fasten off, leaving long tail for sewing, sew hole closed by pulling yarn tail through front loops of remaining sts.

Bring yarn tail to center of Y-shape foot (see Photo 1).

Legs (make 2)

Rnd 1: using Dark Yellow, sc 6 in a magic ring. (6 sts)

Rnds 2 and 3 (2 rnds): sc 1 in each st.

Rnd 4: change to Dark Gray, inc 6 times. (12 sts)

Rnds 5 and 6 (2 rnds): sc 1 in each st.

Fasten off, leaving long tail for sewing.

Stuff firmly.

Sew center of feet to legs. Sew legs to front of body between Rnds 8 and 11, 6 sts apart. Olivia the Owl should be able to sit on a flat surface.

Left wing

Rnd 1: using Dark Gray, sc 6 in a magic ring. (6 sts)

Rnd 2: inc 6 times. (12 sts)

Rnd 3: [sc 1, inc] 6 times. (18 sts)

Rnd 4: [sc 2, inc] 6 times. (24 sts)

Rnd 5: [sc 3, inc] 6 times. (30 sts)

Do not stuff. Fold wing in half and work next row through both layers to close (see Techniques: Closing With Single Crochet).

WHEN CHANGING TO DARK YELLOW, LEAVE DARK GRAY AT THE FRONT OF THE WORK.

Row 6: sc 8, change to Dark Yellow, [sc 1, dc 3 in same st] 3 times, sc 1. (21 sts)

Fasten off Dark Gray and leave a long tail for sewing. Fasten off Dark Yellow and weave in yarn end.

Bring yarn tail to opposite corner of left wing (see Photo 2).

Right wing

Work as for left wing from Rnds 1–5.

Do not stuff. Fold wing in half and work next row through both layers to close.

Row 6: change to Dark Yellow, [sc 1, dc 3 in same st] 3 times, sc 1, change to Dark Gray, sc 8. (21 sts)

Fasten off, leaving long tail for sewing.

Sew wings on corresponding side of body between Rnds 18 and 22, with "feathers" facing towards back and down. Sew only portion of wings between sewing pins as shown (see Photo 3).

Tail

Leave a long tail at beginning of chain for sewing later.

Using Dark Gray, ch 12, join to first ch with slst 1 to make a chain ring, ch 1, start next rnd in same st.

Rnd 1: sc 1 in each ch. (12 sts)

Rnd 2: sc 1 in each st.

Rnd 3: [sc 5, inc] twice. (14 sts)

Rnd 4: sc 1 in each st.

Do not stuff. Flatten opening and work next row through both layers to close.

Row 5: change to Dark Yellow, [sc 1, dc 3 in same st] 3 times, sc 1. (13 sts)

Fasten off and weave in yarn end.

Sew tail to back of body on Rnd 8 (see Photo 4).

Hat

Rnd 1: using White, sc 6 in a magic ring. (6 sts)

Rnd 2: [sc 1, inc] 3 times. (9 sts)

Rnds 3 and 4 (2 rnds): sc 1 in each st.

Rnd 5: [sc 1, inc, sc 1] 3 times. (12 sts)

Rnds 6 and 7 (2 rnds): sc 1 in each st.

Rnd 8: [sc 3, inc] 3 times. (15 sts)

Rnds 9 and 10 (2 rnds): change to Dark Yellow, sc 1 in each st.

Rnd 11: change to White, [sc 2, inc, sc 2] 3 times. (18 sts)

Rnds 12 and 13 (2 rnds): change to Dark Yellow, sc 1 in each st.

Rnd 14: change to Dark Orange, working in FLO, [hdc 2, hdc 2 in same st] 6 times. (24 sts)

Fasten off invisibly, leaving long tail for sewing (see Techniques: Invisible Fasten Off).

Using Dark Orange, make a small pompom and attach to top of hat.

Stuff hat firmly. Sew hat to top of head using unworked loops of Rnd 13.

Jack-o'-lantern

Start by making pumpkin and stem separately.

PUMPKIN

Rnd 1: using Dark Orange, sc 6 in a magic ring. (6 sts)

Rnd 2: inc 6 times. (12 sts)

Rnd 3: [sc 1, inc] 6 times. (18 sts)

Rnd 4: [sc 2, inc] 6 times. (24 sts)

Rnd 5: [sc 3, inc] 6 times. (30 sts)

Rnd 6: [sc 4, inc] 6 times. (36 sts)

Rnds 7–14 (8 rnds): sc 1 in each st.

Start stuffing, cont as you work.

Rnd 15: [sc 4, dec] 6 times. (30 sts)

Rnd 16: [sc 3, dec] 6 times. (24 sts)

Rnd 17: [sc 2, dec] 6 times. (18 sts)

Rnd 18: [sc 1, dec] 6 times. (12 sts)

Rnd 19: dec 6 times. (6 sts)

Fasten off, leaving long tail for sewing and shaping, sew hole closed by pulling yarn tail through front loops of remaining sts.

Using yarn needle, run yarn tail through middle of pumpkin and exit through magic ring (see Photo 5). Insert yarn needle up through bottom, exit through magic ring again, pull tightly to create indentation on side (see Photo 6). Rep five more times to make six indentations total. Weave in yarn end.

STEM

Row 1: using Dark Yellow, ch 4, start in 2nd ch from hook working in back bump of ch, sc 3. (3 sts)

Fasten off, leaving long tail for sewing.

Sew stem to top of pumpkin.

Using Dark Gray, embroider jack-o'-lantern face with straight stitch. Make three vertical lines for each eye over Rnds 10 and 11, 6 sts apart. Make an inverted "V" between eyes on Rnd 11 for nose. Make a zigzag line on Rnd 13 for mouth.

NOVEMBER

Finn Fox & Barnaby Badger

Finn and Barnaby eagerly wait all year long to see the first leaf fall from the tree in their shared garden. They both love to dress in their coziest outfits and enjoy the crispy wind and crunchy leaves while sipping a hot cup of tea.

FINN
15CM (6IN)

BARNABY
14.5CM (5¾IN)

DIFFICULTY LEVEL 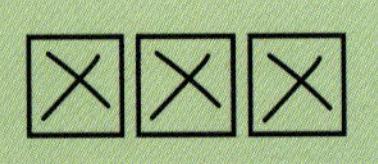

PATTERN NOTES

Most pieces are worked in a spiral without joining each round. The scarf and cardigan body are worked in rows, the cardigan sleeves in closed rounds. Finn is slightly less Advanced in level.

YOU WILL NEED

YARNS:

Hobbii Friends Cotton 8/4 (100% cotton) fingering (4-ply) weight, 160m (174yd) per 50g (1¾oz) ball, in the following shades:

FOR BOTH
- ✓ **White:** 1 ball in White (01)
- ✓ **Deep Pink:** 1 ball in Pink Berry Smoothie (54)
- ✓ **Dark Brown:** 1 ball in Chestnut (11)

FOR FINN
- ✓ **Rust:** 1 ball in Cognac (17)
- ✓ **Mustard:** 1 ball in Mustard (28)
- ✓ **Dark Red:** 1 ball in Cranberry (42)
- ✓ **Sage:** 1 ball in Sage (114)

FOR BARNABY
- ✓ **Dark Gray:** 1 ball in Charcoal (123)
- ✓ **Dark Green:** 1 ball in Hunter Green (116)
- ✓ **Bordeaux:** 1 ball in Bordeaux (43)
- ✓ **Beige:** 1 ball in Beige (05)

HOOK:

- ✓ 2.20mm (US B/1) crochet hook

TOOLS AND MATERIALS:

- ✓ 2 pairs of 8mm safety eyes
- ✓ Stitch markers
- ✓ Yarn needle
- ✓ Toy stuffing
- ✓ 1.5mm gold craft wire or ready-made doll glasses
- ✓ Craft glue (optional)

Finn

Head

Rnd 1: using Rust, sc 6 in a magic ring. (6 sts)

Rnd 2: inc 6 times. (12 sts)

Rnd 3: [sc 1, inc] 6 times. (18 sts)

Rnd 4: [sc 2, inc] 6 times. (24 sts)

Rnd 5: [sc 3, inc] 6 times. (30 sts)

Rnd 6: [sc 4, inc] 6 times. (36 sts)

Rnd 7: [sc 5, inc] 6 times. (42 sts)

Rnd 8: [sc 6, inc] 6 times. (48 sts)

Rnds 9–12 (4 rnds): sc 1 in each st.

Rnd 13: [sc 15, inc] 3 times. (51 sts)

Rnd 14: [sc 8, inc, sc 8] 3 times. (54 sts)

Rnds 15 and 16 (2 rnds): sc 1 in each st.

Rnd 17: sc 11, [inc, sc 1] 3 times, sc 21, [inc, sc 1] 3 times, sc 10 (60 sts)

Rnd 18: change to White, sc 13, [inc, sc 2] 3 times, sc 18, [inc, sc 2] 3 times, sc 11 (66 sts)

Rnds 19 and 20 (2 rnds): sc 1 in each st.

Rnd 21: sc 11, dec 6 times, sc 20, dec 6 times, sc 11. (54 sts)

Rnd 22: [sc 7, dec] 6 times. (48 sts)

Rnd 23: [sc 6, dec] 6 times. (42 sts)

Rnd 24: [sc 5, dec] 6 times. (36 sts)

Place safety eyes between Rnds 15 and 16, 10 sts apart. First eye should be between 21st and 22nd sts and 2nd between 31st and 32nd sts.

Start stuffing, cont as you work.

Rnd 25: [sc 4, dec] 6 times. (30 sts)

Rnd 26: [sc 3, dec] 6 times. (24 sts)

Rnd 27: [sc 2, dec] 6 times. (18 sts)

Rnd 28: [sc 1, dec] 6 times. (12 sts)

Rnd 29: dec around. (6 sts)

Fasten off, sew hole closed by pulling yarn tail through front loops of remaining sts.

Using White and straight stitch (see Techniques: Straight Stitch), make two diagonal lines for each eyebrow on Rnd 13, 2 sts wide.

Muzzle

Rnd 1: using White, sc 6 in a magic ring. (6 sts)

Rnd 2: inc 6 times. (12 sts)

Cont alternating from White to Rust to make muzzle patch.

Rnd 3: (White) sc 3, *sc 1, (Rust) sc 1* in same st, sc 3, *sc 1, (White) sc 1* in same st, sc 3, inc. (15 sts)

Rnd 4: (White) sc 2, inc, sc 1, (Rust) sc 3, inc, sc 1, (White) sc 3, inc, sc 2. (18 sts)

Rnd 5: (White) sc 5, (Rust) sc 6, (White) sc 7. (18 sts)

Fasten off, leaving long tails of White and Rust for sewing.

Using Dark Brown, embroider nose on muzzle. Make six horizontal lines between Rnds 2 and 3, 5 sts wide, and a vertical line centered with nose over 3 rnds.

Sew muzzle to the head centered with eyes between Rnds 15 and 20. Stuff as you sew.

Cheeks (make 2)

Rnd 1: using Deep Pink, sc 6 in a magic ring. (6 sts)

Rnd 2: inc 6 times. (12 sts)

Fasten off invisibly, leaving long tail for sewing (see Techniques: Invisible Fasten Off).

Sew cheeks next to eyes between Rnds 16 and 19.

Ears (make 2)

Rnd 1: using Dark Brown, sc 6 in a magic ring. (6 sts)

Rnd 2: [sc 1, inc] 3 times. (9 sts)

Rnd 3: [sc 1, inc, sc 1] 3 times. (12 sts)

Cont alternating from Dark Brown to Rust.

Rnd 4: [(Dark Brown) sc 1, (Rust) sc 1] 6 times. (12 sts)

Cont working in Rust only.

Rnd 5: [sc 3, inc] 3 times. (15 sts)

Rnd 6: [sc 2, inc, sc 2] 3 times. (18 sts)

Rnds 7–9 (3 rnds): sc 1 in each st.

Fasten off, leaving long tail for sewing.

Do not stuff.

Using White, embroider three double lines on each ear through same st at bottom to make ear tuft.

Flatten ears and sew on each side of head between Rnds 5 and 10 in a curved position.

Legs and body

LEG 1

Rnd 1: using Dark Brown, sc 6 in a magic ring. (6 sts)

Rnd 2: inc 6 times. (12 sts)

Rnds 3–5 (3 rnds): sc 1 in each st.

Rnd 6: change to Dark Red, slst 1 in each st loosely. (12 sts)

Rnd 7: working in BLO of Rnd 6 and both loops of Rnd 5 (see Techniques: Straight Stripe Color Change), sc 1 in each st. (12 sts)

Rnd 8: sc 1 in each st.

Rnd 9: [sc 5, inc] twice. (14 sts)

Rnds 10–12 (3 rnds): sc 1 in each st.

Fasten off. Set aside.

LEG 2

Work as for leg 1, but do not fasten off at end. Cont working on body.

IF NECESSARY, ADD A FEW MORE STITCHES ON LEG 2 TO SHIFT THE COLOR CHANGE TO THE BACK OF THE LEG.

BODY

Rnd 13: still with leg 2 on hook, ch 2, sc 1 in last st of leg 1 to join (see Techniques: Joining Legs), PM here for new beg of rnd, sc 1 in each st of leg 1, inc in each ch, sc 1 in each st of leg 2, inc in each ch. (36 sts)

Stuff legs firmly.

Rnds 14–17 (4 rnds): sc 1 in each st.

Rnd 18: change to Sage, slst 1 in each st loosely.

Rnd 19: work in BLO of rnd 18 and both loops of rnd 17, sc 1 in each st. (36 sts)

Rnd 20: sc 1 in each st.

Rnd 21: [sc 5, dec, sc 5] 3 times. (33 sts)

Rnds 22 and 23 (2 rnds): sc 1 in each st.

Rnd 24: [sc 9, dec] 3 times. (30 sts)

Rnds 25 and 26 (2 rnds): sc 1 in each st.

Rnd 27: [sc 4, dec, sc 4] 3 times. (27 sts)

Rnds 28 and 29 (2 rnds): sc 1 in each st.

Rnd 30: [sc 7, dec] 3 times. (24 sts)

Fasten off, leaving long tail for sewing.

DO NOT STUFF THE BODY IMMEDIATELY TO MAKE ADDING THE SWEATER CABLE KNIT DETAIL EASIER.

Using Mustard, embroider knee patches on legs. Make three horizontal lines on each leg between Rnds 9 and 10, 3 sts wide.

PANT HEM DETAIL

Hold body with legs up and join Dark Red to first unworked loop of Rnd 6 with slst 1 (counts as first st of next rnd) (see Techniques: Joining Yarn to Add a Detail).

Rnd 1: slst 1 in each st. (12 sts)

Fasten off invisibly and weave in yarn ends.

SWEATER HEM DETAIL

Hold body with legs up and join Sage to first unworked loop of Rnd 18 with slst 1 (does not count as a st). Start next rnd in same st.

Rnd 1: sc 1 in each st. (36 sts)

Fasten off invisibly and weave in yarn ends.

SWEATER CABLE KNIT DETAIL

Using Sage, create cable knit effect on body from Rnds 20–28 with surface slst (see Techniques: Surface Slip Stitch). Use sewing pins to plan path of sts as shown (see Photo 1). Alternatively, use a fabric pen to trace path. Make crossing lines centered with legs and two vertical lines on each side (see Photo 2).

Stuff body firmly.

Sew body to bottom of head.

Arms (make 2)

Rnd 1: using Rust, sc 5 in a magic ring. (5 sts)

Rnd 2: inc 5 times. (10 sts)

Rnds 3–5 (3 rnds): sc 1 in each st.

Rnd 6: change to Sage, slst 1 in each st loosely.

Rnd 7: working in BLO of Rnd 6 and both loops of Rnd 5, sc 1 in each st. (10 sts)

Rnds 8–16 (9 rnds): sc 1 in each st.

Stuff lightly. Flatten opening and work next row through both layers to close (see Techniques: Closing with Single Crochet).

Row 17: sc 5. (5 sts)

Fasten off, leaving long tail for sewing.

SWEATER CUFF DETAIL

Hold arm with hand up and join Sage to first unworked loop of Rnd 6 with slst 1 (does not count as a st). Start next rnd in same st.

Rnd 1: sc 1 in each st. (10 sts)

Fasten off invisibly and weave in yarn ends.

Sew arms on each side of body between Rnds 29 and 30.

Tail

Rnd 1: using White, sc 6 in a magic ring. (6 sts)

Rnd 2: [sc 1, inc] 3 times. (9 sts)

Rnd 3: [sc 1, inc, sc 1] 3 times. (12 sts)

Rnd 4: [sc 3, inc] 3 times. (15 sts)

Rnd 5: [sc 2, inc, sc 2] 3 times. (18 sts)

Rnd 6: [sc 5, inc] 3 times. (21 sts)

Rnd 7: [sc 3, inc, sc 3] 3 times. (24 sts)

Rnd 8: [sc 7, inc] 3 times. (27 sts)

Rnd 9: [sc 4, inc, sc 4] 3 times. (30 sts)

Rnd 10: sc 1 in each st.

Cont alternating from White to Rust.

Rnd 11: [(White) sc 2, (Rust) sc 1] 10 times. (30 sts)

Rnd 12: [(White) sc 1, (Rust) sc 2] 10 times. (30 sts)

Cont working in Rust only.

Rnd 13: sc 1 in each st.

Rnd 14: [sc 4, dec, sc 4] 3 times. (27 sts)

Rnd 15: sc 1 in each st.

Start stuffing, cont as you work.

Rnd 16: [sc 7, dec] 3 times. (24 sts)

Rnd 17: sc 1 in each st.

Rnd 18: [sc 3, dec, sc 3] 3 times. (21 sts)

Rnd 19: sc 1 in each st.

Rnd 20: [sc 5, dec] 3 times. (18 sts)

Rnd 21: [sc 2, dec, sc 2] 3 times. (15 sts)

Rnd 22: sc 1 in each st.

Rnd 23: [sc 3, dec] 3 times. (12 sts)

Rnd 24: [sc 1, dec, sc 1] 3 times. (9 sts)

Finish stuffing. Flatten opening and work next row through both layers to close.

Row 25: sc 4, leave 1 sts unworked. (4 sts)

Fasten off, leaving long tail for sewing.

Sew tail to back of body between Rnds 15 and 16 (see Photo 3).

Scarf

Row 1: using Mustard, ch 102, start in 3rd ch from hook working in back bump of ch, hdc 99, [hdc 1, ch 2, slst 1] in last ch. (101 sts)

Fasten off and weave in yarn ends.

Wrap scarf below Finn the Fox's head.

8	9 International Men's Day	10

Barnaby

Eye patches (make 2)

Row 1: using Dark Gray, ch 3, start in 2nd ch from hook working in back bump of ch, sc 2, turn. (2 sts)

Row 2: ch 1, inc twice, turn. (4 sts)

Rows 3 and 4 (2 rows): ch 1, sc 4, turn. (4 sts)

Row 5: ch 1, sc 3, inc, turn. (5 sts)

Rows 6 and 7 (2 rows): ch 1, sc 5, turn. (5 sts)

Row 8: ch 1, sc 4, inc, turn. (6 sts)

Rows 9 and 10 (2 rows): ch 1, sc 6, turn. (6 sts)

Row 11: ch 1, sc 5, inc, turn. (7 sts)

Rows 12 and 13 (2 rows): ch 1, sc 7, turn. (7 sts)

Row 14: ch 1, sc 6, inc, turn. (8 sts)

Rows 15 and 16 (2 rows): ch 1, sc 8, turn. (8 sts)

Row 17: ch 1, sc 7, inc. (9 sts)

Cont working around eye patch.

Rnd 18: sc 17 on side of rows, sc 2 on other side of ch of Row 1, sc 17 on side of rows. (36 sts)

Slst 1 in next st. Fasten off, leaving long tail for sewing.

Head

Rnd 1: using White, sc 6 in a magic ring. (6 sts)

Rnd 2: inc 6 times. (12 sts)

Rnd 3: [sc 1, inc] 6 times. (18 sts)

Rnd 4: [sc 5, inc] 3 times. (21 sts)

Rnd 5: [sc 3, inc, sc 3] 3 times. (24 sts)

Rnd 6: sc 1 in each st.

Rnd 7: [sc 7, inc] 3 times. (27 sts)

Rnd 8: [sc 4, inc, sc 4] 3 times. (30 sts)

Rnd 9: sc 1 in each st.

Rnd 10: [sc 4, inc] 6 times. (36 sts)

Rnd 11: sc 1 in each st.

Rnd 12: sc 6, inc 3 times, sc 3, [inc, sc 1] 6 times, sc 2, inc 3 times, sc 7. (48 sts)

Rnd 13: sc 1 in each st.

Rnd 14: sc 16, [inc, sc 2] 6 times, sc 14. (54 sts)

Rnd 15: sc 1 in each st.

Rnd 16: sc 17, [inc, sc 3] 6 times, sc 13. (60 sts)

Rnds 17–26 (10 rnds): sc 1 in each st.

Rnd 27: [sc 8, dec] 6 times. (54 sts)

Rnd 28: [sc 7, dec] 6 times. (48 sts)

Rnd 29: [sc 6, dec] 6 times. (42 sts)

Place safety eyes on eye patches between Rows 3 and 4. Insert safety eyes on head between Rnds 11 and 12, on 4th and 9th inc. Secure safety eyes inside head.

Sew eye patches to head between Rnds 8 and 26, 8 sts apart at back, now or after stuffing.

Start stuffing, cont as you work.

Rnd 30: [sc 5, dec] 6 times. (36 sts)

Rnd 31: [sc 4, dec] 6 times. (30 sts)

Rnd 32: [sc 3, dec] 6 times. (24 sts)

Rnd 33: [sc 2, dec] 6 times. (18 sts)

Rnd 34: [sc 1, dec] 6 times. (12 sts)

Rnd 35: dec 6 times. (6 sts)

Fasten off, sew hole closed by pulling yarn tail through front loops of remaining sts.

Embroider face details in straight stitch (see Techniques: Straight Stitch). Using White, make a line on outer side of each eye for depth (see Photo 1).

Using Dark Gray, embroider nose on front of head. Make six horizontal lines between Rnds 2 and 3, 4 sts wide.

Cheeks (make 2)

Rnd 1: using Deep Pink, sc 6 in a magic ring. (6 sts)

Rnd 2: inc 6 times. (12 sts)

Fasten off invisibly, leaving long tail for sewing (see Techniques: Invisible Fasten Off).

Sew cheeks below eye patches between Rnds 14 and 17 (see Photo 1).

Ears (make 2)

Rnd 1: using White, sc 6 in a magic ring. (6 sts)

Rnd 2: inc 6 times. (12 sts)

Rnd 3: [sc 1, inc] 6 times. (18 sts)

Rnds 4–6 (3 rnds): change to Dark Gray, sc 1 in each st.

Fasten off, leaving long tail for sewing.

Do not stuff. Flatten ears into a semi-circle.

Sew ears on top of eye patches on Rows 14 and 15 in a curved position (see Photo 1).

Legs and body

LEG 1

Rnd 1: using Dark Gray, sc 6 in a magic ring. (6 sts)

Rnd 2: inc 6 times. (12 sts)

Rnd 3: [sc 2, inc] 4 times. (16 sts)

Rnds 4–10 (7 rnds): sc 1 in each st.

Fasten off. Set aside.

LEG 2

Work as for leg 1, but do not fasten off at end. Cont working on body.

BODY

Rnd 11: still with leg 2 on hook, ch 2, sc 1 in first st of leg 1 to join (see Techniques: Joining Legs), PM here for new beg of rnd, sc 1 in each st of leg 1, inc in each ch, sc 1 in each st of leg 2, inc in each ch. (40 sts)

Rnds 12 and 13 (2 rnds): sc 1 in each st.

Stuff legs firmly.

Rnd 14: [sc 9, inc] 4 times. (44 sts)

Rnds 15–17 (3 rnds): sc 1 in each st.

Rnd 18: change to Dark Green, slst 1 in each st loosely.

Rnd 19: working in BLO of Rnd 18 and both loops of Rnd 17 (see Techniques: Straight Stripe Color Change), sc 1 in each st. (44 sts)

Rnds 20 and 21 (2 rnds): sc 1 in each st.

Rnd 22: [sc 9, dec] 4 times. (40 sts)

Rnds 23 and 24 (2 rnds): sc 1 in each st.

Rnd 25: [sc 4, dec, sc 4] 4 times. (36 sts)

Rnds 26 and 27 (2 rnds): sc 1 in each st.

Rnd 28: [sc 5, dec, sc 5] 3 times. (33 sts)

Rnds 29 and 30 (2 rnds): sc 1 in each st.

Rnd 31: [sc 9, dec] 3 times. (30 sts)

Rnd 32: [sc 3, dec] 6 times, turn. (24 sts)

Cont working in opposite direction.

Rnd 33: ch 2, work in BLO, dc 11, ch 3, slst 1, ch 3, dc 12, slst 1 to first st to join. (24 sts)

IF NECESSARY, ADJUST THE POSITION OF THE COLLAR'S SPLIT TO ALIGN WITH THE GAP BETWEEN THE LEGS.

Fasten off, leaving long tail for sewing.

Stuff body firmly.

SHIRT HEM DETAIL

Hold body with legs up and join Dark Green to first unworked loop of Rnd 18 with slst 1 (counts as first st of next rnd).

Rnd 1: slst 1 in each st. (44 sts)

Fasten off invisibly and weave in yarn ends.

Sew body to bottom of head between Rnds 14 and 22 using unworked loops from Rnd 32 of body.

Arms (make 2)

Rnd 1: using Dark Gray, sc 6 in a magic ring. (6 sts)

Rnd 2: inc 6 times. (12 sts)

Rnds 3–5 (3 rnds): sc 1 in each st.

Rnd 6: change to Dark Green, slst 1 in each st loosely.

Rnd 7: work in BLO of rnd 6 and both loops of rnd 5, sc 1 in each st. (12 sts)

Rnds 8–17 (10 rnds): sc 1 in each st.

Stuff lightly. Flatten opening and work next row through both layers to close (see Techniques: Closing with Single Crochet).

Row 18: sc 6. (6 sts)

Fasten off, leaving long tail for sewing.

SHIRT CUFF DETAIL

Hold arm with hand up and join Dark Green to first unworked loop of Rnd 6 with slst 1 (does not count as a st). Start next rnd in same st.

Rnd 1: slst 1 in each st. (12 sts)

Fasten off invisibly and weave in yarn ends.

Sew arms on each side of body between Rnds 31 and 32.

Tail

Rnd 1: using White, sc 6 in a magic ring. (6 sts)

Rnd 2: [sc 1, inc] 3 times. (9 sts)

Rnds 3 and 4 (2 rnds): sc 1 in each st.

Rnd 5: [sc 1, inc, sc 1] 3 times. (12 sts)

Rnds 6–10 (5 rnds): change to Dark Gray, sc 1 in each st.

Stuff lightly. Flatten opening and work next row through both layers to close.

Row 11: sc 6. (6 sts)

Fasten off, leaving long tail for sewing.

Sew tail to back of body between Rnds 15 and 16 (see Photo 2).

Pants

Start by making the pant legs.

PANT LEG 1

Using Dark Brown, ch 24, join to first ch with slst 1 to make a chain ring, ch 1, start next rnd in same st.

Rnd 1: sc 1 in each ch working in back bump of ch. (24 sts)

Rnds 2 and 3 (2 rnds): sc 1 in each st.

Cont alternating from Dark Brown to Beige to make plaid pattern.

Rnds 4 and 5 (2 rnds): [(Dark Brown) sc 2, (Beige) sc 1] 8 times. (24 sts)

Rnd 6: (Beige) sc 1 in each st.

Rnd 7: [(Dark Brown) sc 2, (Beige) sc 1] 8 times. (24 sts)

Fasten off. Set aside.

PANT LEG 2

Work as for leg 1, but do not fasten off at end. Cont working on pants.

JOINING THE PANT LEGS

Rnd 8: still with leg 2 on hook, (Dark Brown) sc 1 in first st of leg 1 to join, PM here for new beg of rnd, sc 1, (Beige) sc 1, [(Dark Brown) sc 2, (Beige) sc 1] 7 times on leg 1, [(Dark Brown) sc 2, (Beige) sc 1] 8 times on leg 2. (48 sts)

Rnd 9: (Beige) sc 1 in each st.

Rnds 10 and 11 (2 rnds): [(Dark Brown) sc 2, (Beige) sc 1] 16 times. (48 sts)

IF NECESSARY, ADJUST THE POSITION OF THE CHAIN FOR THE HOLE FOR THE TAIL, MAKING SURE IT'S CENTERED AT THE BACK OF THE PANTS.

Rnd 12: (Beige) sc 45, (Dark Brown) ch 6 and skip 3 sts. (45 sts + 6 chs)

Rnd 13: skip 3 sts, [(Dark Brown) sc 2, (Beige) sc 1] 14 times, [(Dark Brown) sc 2, (Beige) sc 1] on ch. (45 sts)

Rnd 14: [(Dark Brown) sc 2, (Beige) sc 1] on the ch, [(Dark Brown) sc 2, (Beige) sc 1] 15 times. (48 sts)

Rnd 15: [(Beige) sc 10, dec] 4 times. (44 sts)

Cont working in Dark Brown only.

Rnd 16: sc 1 in each st.

Fasten off invisibly and weave in yarn ends.

Fold first two rnds of each leg up.

Place pants on Barnaby the Badger, with tail through gap on back.

Cardigan

Start by making body and sleeves separately.

BODY

Row 1: using Bordeaux, ch 30, start in 3rd ch from hook working in back bump of ch, hdc 28, turn. (28 sts)

Row 2: ch 2, [hdc 6, hdc 2 in same st] 4 times, turn. (32 sts)

Row 3: ch 2, [hdc 7, hdc 2 in same st] 4 times, turn. (36 sts)

Row 4: ch 2, hdc 2 in same st, hdc 2, ch 7, skip 6 sts, hdc 18, ch 7, skip 6 sts, hdc 2, hdc 2 in same st, turn. (26 sts + 14 chs)

Row 5: ch 2, hdc 4, hdc 7 on ch, hdc 18, hdc 7 on ch, hdc 4, turn. (40 sts)

Row 6: ch 2, hdc 40, turn. (40 sts)

Row 7: ch 2, [hdc 9, hdc 2 in same st] 4 times. (44 sts)

Rows 8 and 9 (2 rows): ch 2, hdc 44, turn. (44 sts)

Row 10: ch 2, hdc 44. (44 sts)

Cont working around body of cardigan.

Rnd 11: ch 1, working on side of rows, sc 9, hdc 5, hdc 2 in same st, working on foundation ch, hdc 28, working on side of rows, hdc 2 in same st, hdc 5, sc 9. (60 sts)

Slst 1 in next st. Fasten off and weave in yarn ends.

LEFT SLEEVE

The sleeves are worked in closed rnds. Start each rnd with ch 2, end with slst 1 on first st to join.

Hold cardigan body up and join Bordeaux to right side of gap (see Photo 3) on Row 4 with slst 1 (does not count as a st) (see Techniques: Joining Yarn to Add a Detail). Start next rnd in same st.

Rnd 1: ch 2, hdc 1 on side of gap, hdc 7 on ch, hdc 1 on side of gap, hdc 6 on Row 3, slst 1 to first st to join. (15 sts)

Rnds 2–4 (3 rnds): ch 2, hdc 1 in each st, slst 1 to first st to join. (15 sts)

Fasten off and weave in yarn ends.

RIGHT SLEEVE

Hold cardigan body upside down and join Bordeaux to right side of the gap on Row 4 with slst 1 (does not count as a st). Start next rnd in same st.

Rnd 1: ch 2, hdc 1 on side of gap, hdc 6 on Row 3, hdc 1 on side of gap, hdc 7 on ch, slst 1 to first st to join. (15 sts)

Rnds 2–4 (3 rnds): ch 2, hdc 1 in each st, slst 1 to first st to join. (15 sts)

Fasten off and weave in yarn ends (see Photo 4).

Place cardigan on Barnaby the Badger.

Glasses

Using gold craft wire, create glasses for Barnaby the Badger (see Techniques: Making Doll Glasses). Alternatively, use ready-made doll glasses. Attach glasses to top of head between eyes with craft glue or a few sewn stitches using White (see Photo 5).

DECEMBER

Riley Reindeer & Mason Mouse

Mason and Riley's favorite holiday is coming up and they've already put up a Christmas tree, covered in handmade baubles and shining lights – it looks like Riley might have some lights tangled on his antlers! As for Mason, he's been assigned the most important task, helping Santa Claus deliver gifts.

RILEY
15CM (6IN)

MASON
14.5CM (5¾IN)

PATTERN NOTES

Most pieces are worked in a spiral without joining each round. The scarf, hooded cape, and bib of the overalls are worked in rows.

DIFFICULTY LEVEL ☒☒☐

YOU WILL NEED

YARNS:

Hobbii Friends Cotton 8/4 (100% cotton) fingering (4-ply) weight, 160m (174yd) per 50g (1¾oz) ball, in the following shades:

FOR BOTH

✓ **Red:** 1 ball in Tomato (40)
✓ **Bright Green:** 1 ball in Jungle Green (111)

FOR RILEY

✓ **Brown:** 1 ball in Cappuccino (10)
✓ **Dark Brown:** 1 ball in Chestnut (11)
✓ **Cream:** 1 ball in Oatmilk (03)
✓ **Dark Yellow:** 1 ball in Dark Yellow (26)

FOR MASON

✓ **Beige:** 1 ball in Beige (05)
✓ **White:** 1 ball in White (01)
✓ **Pale Pink:** 1 ball in Rose (44)
✓ **Mustard:** 1 ball in Mustard (28)

HOOK:

✓ 2.20mm (US B/1) crochet hook

TOOLS AND MATERIALS:

✓ 1 pair of 8mm safety eyes
✓ 1 pair of 6mm safety eyes
✓ Stitch markers
✓ Yarn needle
✓ Toy stuffing

Riley

Head

Rnd 1: using Brown, sc 6 in a magic ring. (6 sts)

Rnd 2: inc 6 times. (12 sts)

Rnd 3: [sc 1, inc] 6 times. (18 sts)

Rnd 4: [sc 2, inc] 6 times. (24 sts)

Rnd 5: [sc 3, inc] 6 times. (30 sts)

Rnd 6: [sc 4, inc] 6 times. (36 sts)

Rnd 7: [sc 5, inc] 6 times. (42 sts)

Rnd 8: [sc 6, inc] 6 times. (48 sts)

Rnds 9–14 (6 rnds): sc 1 in each st.

Rnd 15: sc 9, [inc, sc 2] 3 times, sc 12, [inc, sc 2] 3 times, sc 9. (54 sts)

Rnds 16–19 (4 rnds): sc 1 in each st.

Rnd 20: [sc 7, dec] 6 times. (48 sts)

Rnd 21: [sc 6, dec] 6 times. (42 sts)

Rnd 22: [sc 5, dec] 6 times. (36 sts)

Place 8mm safety eyes between Rnds 14 and 15, 10 sts apart. First eye should be between 18th and 19th sts of Rnd 14 and 2nd between 28th and 29th sts.

Start stuffing, cont as you work.

Rnd 23: [sc 4, dec] 6 times. (30 sts)

Rnd 24: [sc 3, dec] 6 times. (24 sts)

Rnd 25: [sc 2, dec] 6 times. (18 sts)

Rnd 26: [sc 1, dec] 6 times. (12 sts)

Rnd 27: dec 6 times. (6 sts)

Fasten off, sew hole closed by pulling yarn tail through front loops of remaining sts.

Using Cream, embroider eyebrows in straight stitch (see Techniques: Straight Stitch). Make two diagonal lines on Rnd 12 above eyes, 2 sts wide.

Muzzle

Rnd 1: using Cream, sc 6 in a magic ring. (6 sts)

Rnd 2: inc 6 times. (12 sts)

Rnd 3: [sc 1, inc] 6 times. (18 sts)

Rnd 4: [sc 5, inc] 3 times. (21 sts)

Rnds 5 and 6 (2 rnds): sc 1 in each st.

Fasten off, leaving long tail for sewing.

Sew muzzle to the head centered with eyes between Rnds 14 and 20. Stuff as you sew.

Nose

Rnd 1: using Red, sc 5 in a magic ring. (5 sts)

Rnd 2: inc 5 times. (10 sts)

Rnds 3 and 4 (2 rnds): sc 1 in each st.

Fasten off, leaving long tail for sewing.

Stuff lightly.

Sew nose on muzzle between Rnds 3 and 5.

Cheeks (make 2)

Rnd 1: using Red, sc 6 in a magic ring. (6 sts)

Rnd 2: inc 6 times. (12 sts)

Fasten off invisibly, leaving long tail for sewing (see Techniques: Invisible Fasten Off).

Sew cheeks next to eyes between Rnds 15 and 18.

Antlers (make 2)

Start by making tines of antlers.

SMALL TINES (MAKE 2 FOR EACH ANTLER)

Rnd 1: using Cream, sc 6 in a magic ring. (6 sts)

Rnds 2–4 (3 rnds): sc 1 in each st.

Fasten off and weave in yarn end. Set aside.

Stuff firmly.

LONG TINES (MAKE 1 FOR EACH ANTLER)

Rnd 1: using Cream, sc 6 in a magic ring. (6 sts)

Rnd 2: [sc 1, inc] 3 times. (9 sts)

Rnds 3–7 (5 rnds): sc 1 in each st.

Do not fasten off. Stuff firmly.

Cont joining tines.

JOINING THE TINES

Rnd 8: still with long tine on hook, sc 1 in last st of small tine to join, PM here for new beg of rnd, sc 1 in each st of small tine (see Photo 1), sc 1 in each st of long tine. (15 sts)

Rnd 9: [sc 3, dec] 3 times. (12 sts)

Start stuffing, cont as you work.

Rnd 10: [sc 2, dec] 3 times. (9 sts)

Rnd 11: sc 1 in each st.

IF NECESSARY, ADJUST THE POSITION OF THE 2ND SMALL TINE TO GUARANTEE IT IS FACING THE OPPOSITE SIDE TO THE FIRST SMALL TINE.

Rnd 12: sc 7, sc 1 in last st of small tine to join, sc 1 in each st of small tine, sc 2. (15 sts)

Rnd 13: [sc 3, dec] 3 times. (12 sts)

Rnd 14: [sc 2, dec] 3 times. (9 sts)

Rnds 15–17 (3 rnds): sc 1 in each st.

Fasten off, leaving long tail for sewing.

Sew antlers on each side of head between Rnds 5 and 7, with 2nd small tine pointing upwards.

Ears (make 2)

Rnd 1: using Brown, sc 6 in a magic ring. (6 sts)

Rnd 2: [sc 1, inc] 3 times. (9 sts)

Rnd 3: sc 1 in each st.

Rnd 4: [sc 1, inc, sc 1] 3 times. (12 sts)

Rnds 5 and 6 (2 rnds): sc 1 in each st.

Rnd 7: [sc 1, dec] 4 times. (8 sts)

Do not stuff. Flatten opening and work next row through both layers to close (see Techniques: Closing with Single Crochet).

Row 8: sc 4. (4 sts)

Fasten off, leaving long tail for sewing.

Flatten ears in opposite direction of last row. Sew ears below antlers between Rnds 8 and 9.

Front legs (make 2)

Rnd 1: using Dark Brown, sc 6 in a magic ring. (6 sts)

Rnd 2: inc 6 times. (12 sts)

Rnds 3–5 (3 rnds): sc 1 in each st.

Rnds 6–13 (8 rnds): change to Brown, sc 1 in each st.

Fasten off, leaving long tail for sewing.

Stuff lightly.

Body

Rnd 1: using Brown, sc 6 in a magic ring. (6 sts)

Rnd 2: inc 6 times. (12 sts)

Rnd 3: [sc 1, inc] 6 times. (18 sts)

Rnd 4: [sc 2, inc] 6 times. (24 sts)

Rnd 5: [sc 3, inc] 6 times. (30 sts)

Rnd 6: [sc 4, inc] 6 times. (36 sts)

Rnd 7: [sc 5, inc] 6 times. (42 sts)

Rnd 8: [sc 6, inc] 6 times. (48 sts)

Rnd 9: [sc 15, inc] 3 times. (51 sts)

Rnds 10–13 (4 rnds): sc 1 in each st.

Rnd 14: [sc 15, dec] 3 times. (48 sts)

Rnds 15 and 16 (2 rnds): sc 1 in each st.

Rnd 17: [sc 14, dec] 3 times. (45 sts)

Rnd 18: sc 1 in each st.

Front legs are attached in next rnd (see Techniques: Joining Front Legs).

Rnd 19: sc 16 on body, sc 6 on first front leg, skip 6 sts of body and of front leg, sc 1 on body, sc 6 on 2nd front leg, skip 6 sts of body and of front leg, sc 16 on body. (45 sts)

With yarn tail left on front legs, sew unworked sts of front legs to skipped sts of body. Grab only loops on inside where body and front legs are joined. Secure middle of legs to body with a couple of sewn stitches.

Cont working around body and sts worked on front legs on Rnd 19.

Stuff body firmly, cont as you work.

Rnd 20: [sc 13, dec] 3 times. (42 sts)

Rnd 21: sc 1 in each st.

Rnd 22: [sc 6, dec, sc 6] 3 times. (39 sts)

Rnd 23: sc 1 in each st.

Rnd 24: [sc 11, inc] 3 times. (36 sts)

Rnd 25: sc 1 in each st.

Rnd 26: [sc 5, dec, sc 5] 3 times. (33 sts)

Rnd 27: sc 9, dec, sc 1, hdc 8, hdc dec, hdc 1, sc 8, dec. (30 sts)

Fasten off, leaving long tail for sewing.

Sew body to bottom of head, with both front legs touching flat surface, and face facing forward aligned with front legs.

Back legs (make 2)

Rnd 1: using Dark Brown, sc 6 in a magic ring. (6 sts)

Rnd 2: inc 6 times. (12 sts)

Rnds 3–5 (3 rnds): sc 1 in each st.

Rnds 6–8 (3 rnds): change to Brown, sc 1 in each st.

Stuff firmly to here.

Rnd 9: sc 3, inc 6 times, sc 3. (18 sts)

Rnd 10: sc 7, inc 3 times, sc 8. (21 sts)

Rnds 11–14 (4 rnds): sc 1 in each st.

Stuff rest of back legs lightly.

Rnd 15: [sc 5, dec] 3 times. (18 sts)

Rnd 16: [sc 1, dec] 6 times. (12 sts)

Rnd 17: dec 6 times. (6 sts)

Fasten off, leaving long tail for sewing, sew hole closed by pulling yarn tail through front loops of remaining sts.

Sew back legs on each side of body, between Rnds 8 and 13, slightly back from front legs. Riley the Reindeer should be able to sit on a flat surface.

Tail

Rnd 1: using Brown, sc 6 in a magic ring. (6 sts)

Rnd 2: [sc 1, inc] 3 times. (9 sts)

Rnd 3: sc 1 in each st.

Rnd 4: [sc 1, inc, sc 1] 3 times. (12 sts)

Rnds 5–7 (3 rnds): sc 1 in each st.

Stuff lightly.

Rnd 8: dec 6 times. (6 sts)

Fasten off, leaving long tail for sewing, sew hole closed by pulling yarn tail through front loops of remaining sts.

Sew tail to back of body, with magic ring pointing upwards, between Rnds 5 and 7.

Scarf

Row 1: using Bright Green, ch 6, start in 3rd ch from hook working in back bump of ch, hdc 4, turn. (4 sts)

CARRY THE YARN OF THE PREVIOUS COLOR ON TOP OF THE ROW AFTER EACH COLOR CHANGE TO AVOID MULTIPLE YARN ENDS TO WEAVE IN.

Row 2: change to Red, ch 2, hdc 4, turn. (4 sts)

Row 3: change to Bright Green, ch 2, hdc 4, turn. (4 sts)

Rows 4–41 (38 rows): rep Rows 2 and 3 nineteen more times.

Fasten off and weave in yarn ends.

Cut 8 strands of Red 5cm (2in) long. Attach four strands on each short side of scarf (see Techniques: Attaching Yarn Strands). Trim to desired length.

Wrap scarf below Riley the Reindeer's head.

String of lights

Start by making lights and string separately.

LIGHTS (MAKE 3 DARK YELLOW, 2 RED, 2 BRIGHT GREEN)

Rnd 1: using Dark Yellow/Red/Bright Green, sc 6 in a magic ring. (6 sts)

Rnds 2 and 3 (2 rnds): sc 1 in each st.

Do not stuff.

Fasten off, sew hole closed by pulling yarn tail through front loops of remaining sts.

STRING

Row 1: using Dark Brown, [ch 6, sc 1 through top of light] 7 times (see Photos 2 and 3), ch 6. (56 chs + 7 sts)

Fasten off and weave in yarn ends.

Wrap string of lights around antlers.

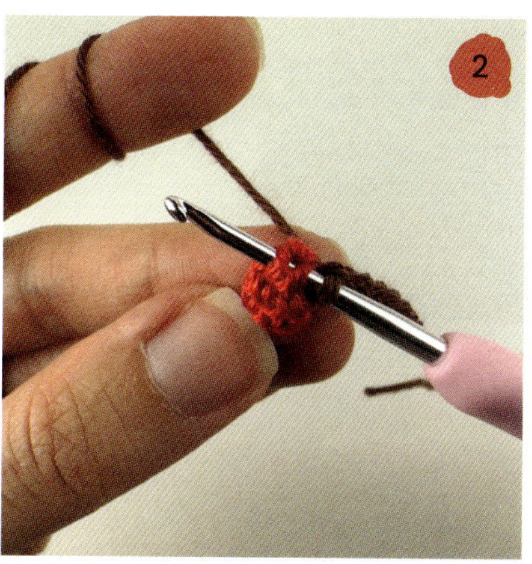

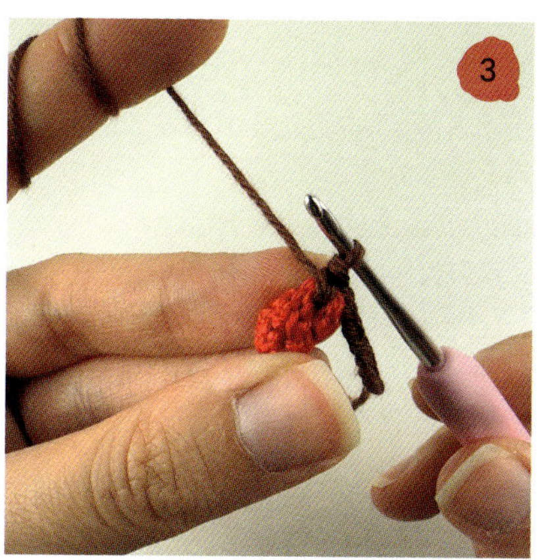

Mason

Head

Rnd 1: using Beige, sc 6 in a magic ring. (6 sts)

Rnd 2: inc 6 times. (12 sts)

Rnd 3: sc 1 in each st.

Rnd 4: [sc 3, inc] 3 times. (15 sts)

Rnd 5: [sc 2, inc, sc 2] 3 times. (18 sts)

Rnd 6: [sc 5, inc] 3 times. (21 sts)

Rnd 7: [sc 3, inc, sc 3] 3 times. (24 sts)

Rnd 8: sc 6, [inc, sc 1] 6 times, sc 6. (30 sts)

Rnd 9: [sc 4, inc] 6 times. (36 sts)

Rnd 10: sc 10, [inc, sc 2] 6 times, sc 8. (42 sts)

Rnd 11: [sc 3, inc, sc 3] 6 times. (48 sts)

Rnd 12: [sc 7, inc] 6 times. (54 sts)

Rnds 13–22 (10 rnds): sc 1 in each st.

Rnd 23: [sc 7, dec] 6 times. (48 sts)

Rnd 24: [sc 6, dec] 6 times. (42 sts)

Place 6mm safety eyes between Rnds 9 and 10, 15 sts apart. First eye should be between 9th and 10th sts of Rnd 9 and 2nd between 24th and 25th sts.

Start stuffing, cont as you work.

Rnd 25: [sc 5, dec] 6 times. (36 sts)

Rnd 26: [sc 4, dec] 6 times. (30 sts)

Rnd 27: [sc 3, dec] 6 times. (24 sts)

Rnd 28: [sc 2, dec] 6 times. (18 sts)

Rnd 29: [sc 1, dec] 6 times. (12 sts)

Rnd 30: dec 6 times. (6 sts)

Fasten off, sew hole closed by pulling yarn tail through front loops of remaining sts.

Using White, embroider eyebrows in straight stitch (see Techniques: Straight Stitch). Make a diagonal line above eyes on Rnd 11 for each eyebrow, 3 sts wide.

Nose

Rnd 1: using Pale Pink, sc 6 in a magic ring. (6 sts)

Rnd 2: sc 1 in each st.

Fasten off, leaving long tail for sewing.

Do not stuff. Sew nose centered with eyes on Rnds 1 and 2.

Using Pale Pink, embroider a vertical line centered with nose, 3 rnds tall.

Cheeks (make 2)

Rnd 1: using Pale Pink, sc 6 in a magic ring. (6 sts)

Rnd 2: inc 6 times. (12 sts)

Fasten off invisibly, leaving long tail for sewing (see Techniques: Invisible Fasten Off).

Sew cheeks next to eyes between Rnds 11 and 14.

Ears (make 2)

Start by making inner layer and outer layer of ears separately.

INNER LAYERS (MAKE 1 FOR EACH EAR)

Rnd 1: using Pale Pink, sc 6 in a magic ring. (6 sts)

Rnd 2: inc 6 times. (12 sts)

Rnd 3: [sc 1, inc] 6 times. (18 sts)

Rnd 4: [sc 1, inc, sc 1] 6 times. (24 sts)

Rnd 5: [sc 3, inc] 6 times. (30 sts)

Fasten off. Set aside.

OUTER LAYERS (MAKE 1 FOR EACH EAR)

Using Beige, work as for inner layer from Rnds 1–5.

Align sts of outer layer with inner layer (wrong sides together), work next rnd through both layers.

Rnd 6: sc 1 in each st. (30 sts)

Rnd 7: slst 1 in each st.

Fasten off, leaving long tail for sewing.

Sew ears on each side of head on Rnd 18, 14 sts apart at top.

Legs and body

LEG 1

Rnd 1: using Pale Pink, sc 6 in a magic ring. (6 sts)

Rnd 2: inc twice, [sc 3 in same st] 3 times, inc. (15 sts)

Rnds 3 and 4 (2 rnds): sc 1 in each st.

Rnd 5: sc 4, dec 3 times, sc 5. (12 sts)

Rnd 6: sc 4, dec twice, sc 4. (10 sts)

Rnd 7: change to Beige, sc 4, inc twice, sc 4. (12 sts)

Rnd 8: sc 1 in each st.

Rnd 9: sc 5, inc twice, sc 5. (14 sts)

Rnds 10 and 11 (2 rnds): sc 1 in each st.

Fasten off. Set aside.

LEG 2

Work as for leg 1, but do not fasten off at end. Cont working on body.

ADD A FEW MORE STITCHES ON LEG 2 TO REACH THE INSIDE OF THE LEG TO KEEP THE FOOT SHAPING FACING FORWARD AND SLIGHTLY TO THE OUTSIDE WHEN JOINING THE LEGS.

BODY

Rnd 12: still with leg 2 on hook, ch 2, sc 1 in 13th st of leg 1 to join (see Techniques: Joining Legs), PM here for new beg of rnd, sc 1 in each st of leg 1, inc in each ch, sc 1 in each st of leg 2, inc in each ch. (36 sts)

Stuff legs firmly.

Rnds 13–16 (4 rnds): sc 1 in each st.

Rnd 17: change to Mustard, slst 1 in each st loosely.

Rnd 18: working in BLO of Rnd 17 and both loops of Rnd 16 (see Techniques: Straight Stripe Color Change), sc 1 in each st. (36 sts)

Rnd 19: sc 1 in each st.

Rnd 20: [sc 5, dec, sc 5] 3 times. (33 sts)

Rnds 21 and 22 (2 rnds): sc 1 in each st.

Rnd 23: [sc 9, dec] 3 times. (30 sts)

Rnd 24: sc 1 in each st.

Rnd 25: [sc 4, dec, sc 4] 3 times. (27 sts)

Rnd 26: sc 1 in each st.

Rnd 27: [sc 7, dec] 3 times. (24 sts)

Fasten off, leaving long tail for sewing.

Stuff body firmly.

SWEATER HEM DETAIL

Hold body with legs up and join Mustard to first unworked loop of Rnd 17 with slst 1 (counts as first st of next rnd).

Rnd 1: slst 1 in each st. (36 sts)

Fasten off invisibly and weave in yarn ends.

Sew body to bottom of head between Rnds 14 and 21.

Arms (make 2)

Rnd 1: using Beige, sc 6 in a magic ring. (6 sts)

Rnd 2: [sc 1, inc] 3 times. (9 sts)

Rnds 3–5 (3 rnds): sc 1 in each st.

Rnd 6: change to Mustard, slst 1 in each st loosely.

Rnd 7: work in BLO of rnd 6 and both loops of rnd 5, sc 1 in each st. (9 sts)

Rnds 8–13 (6 rnds): sc 1 in each st.

Stuff lightly. Flatten opening and work next row through both layers to close (see Techniques: Closing with Single Crochet).

Row 14: sc 4. (4 sts)

Fasten off, leaving long tail for sewing.

SWEATER CUFF DETAIL

Hold arm with hand up and join Mustard to first unworked loop of Rnd 6 with slst 1 (counts as first st of next rnd).

Rnd 1: slst 1 in each st. (9 sts)

Fasten off invisibly and weave in yarn ends.

Sew arms on each side of body between Rnds 26 and 27.

Tail

Row 1: using Pale Pink, ch 16, starting in 2nd ch from hook, slst 15. (15 sts)

Fasten off, leaving long tail for sewing.

Sew tail to back of body on Rnd 15 (see Photo 1).

Overalls

Start by making overall legs and bib separately.

OVERALL LEG 1

Using Bright Green, ch 18, join to first ch with slst 1 to make a chain ring, ch 1, start next rnd in same st.

Rnd 1: sc 1 in each ch working in back bump the ch. (18 sts)

Rnds 2–4 (3 rnds): sc 1 in each st.

Fasten off. Set aside.

OVERALL LEG 2

Work as for overall leg 1, but do not fasten off at end. Cont working on the overalls.

JOINING THE LEGS

Rnd 5: still with leg 2 on hook, ch 1, sc 1 in first st of leg 1 to join, PM here for new beg of rnd, sc 1 in each st of leg 1, inc on ch, sc 1 in each st of leg 2, inc on ch. (40 sts)

Rnds 6 and 7 (2 rnds): sc 1 in each st.

IF NECESSARY, ADJUST THE POSITION OF THE CHAIN FOR THE HOLE FOR THE TAIL, MAKING SURE IT'S CENTERED AT THE BACK OF THE PANTS.

Rnd 8: sc 38, ch 2 and skip 2 sts. (40 sts)

Rnd 9: sc 38, sc 2 on the ch. (40 sts)

Rnds 10 and 11 (2 rnds): sc 1 in each st.

Rnd 12: [sc 8, dec] 4 times. (36 sts)

Rnd 13: sc 8, end rnd here. (8 sts)

Fasten off invisibly and weave in yarn ends.

Fold first two rnds of each leg up.

OVERALL BIB

Identify 9 sts at front of overalls and PM on first and 9th sts.

Hold overalls up and join Bright Green to marked st on right with slst 1 (does not count as a st). Start next row in same st.

Rows 1–4 (4 rows): ch 1, sc 9, turn. (9 sts)

Row 5: ch 1, sc 9. (9 sts)

Cont making straps.

Row 6: ch 15, slst 1 to last st of Rnd 12 of overalls (see Photo 2), ch 15, slst 1 to first st of Row 5 of bib. (30 chs + 2 sts)

Fasten off and weave in yarn ends.

Place overalls on Mason the Mouse, with tail through gap on back and straps over arms.

Hooded cape

Start by making hood and cape separately.

HOOD

Leave a long tail of about 40cm (15in) at beginning of chain for sewing later.

Row 1 (RS): using Red, ch 46, start in 3rd ch from hook working in back bump of ch, hdc 44, turn. (44 sts)

Row 2: change to White, ch 2, hdc 44, turn. (44 sts)

Row 3: change to Red, ch 2, hdc 44, turn. (44 sts)

Rows 4–7 (4 rows): rep rows 2 and 3 twice more.

Row 8: rep Row 2.

Row 9: change to Red, ch 2, hdc 9, ch 7, skip 7 sts, hdc 12, ch 7, skip 7 sts, hdc 9, turn. (30 sts + 14 chs)

Row 10: change to White, ch 2, hdc 9, hdc 7 on ch, hdc 12, hdc 7 on ch, hdc 9, turn. (44 sts)

Row 11: rep Row 3.

Fasten off and weave in yarn ends.

Fold hood in half, right sides facing, perpendicular to direction of rows. Sew both sides of foundation ch with beginning yarn tail (see Photo 3). Weave in yarn end.

Turn hood inside out.

CAPE

Hold hood with opening facing away and join Red to right corner with slst 1 (does not count as a st). Start next row in same st (see Photo 4).

Row 1: ch 1, sc 23 at base of hood, turn. (23 sts)

Row 2: ch 2, working in BLO, hdc 2 in same st, hdc 21, hdc 2 in same st, turn. (25 sts)

Row 3: change to White, ch 2, hdc 2 in same st, hdc 23, hdc 2 in same st, turn. (27 sts)

Row 4: change to Red, ch 2, hdc 2 in same st, hdc 25, hdc 2 in same st, turn. (29 sts)

Row 5: change to White, ch 2, hdc 29. (29 sts)

Fasten off and weave in yarn ends.

Cut 30cm (12in) strand of Red for strap. Run strand through each unworked loop of Row 1 of cape (see Photo 5).

Place hood on Mason the Mouse's head, ears going through gaps, and cape on back. Pull tightly on each end of strand and tie a knot with a bow to secure. Tie a knot on each end of strand to avoid splitting. Trim excess yarn.

Gift box

Start by making lid, box, and ribbon separately.

LID

Rnd 1: using Red, sc 8 in a magic ring. (8 sts)

Rnd 2: [sc 1, sc 3 in same st] 4 times. (16 sts)

Rnd 3: [sc 2, sc 3 in same st, sc 1] 4 times. (24 sts)

Rnd 4: [sc 3, sc 3 in same st, sc 2] 4 times. (32 sts)

Rnd 5: working in BLO, sc 1 in each st. (32 sts)

Rnd 6: sc 1 in each st.

Rnd 7: slst 1 in each st.

Fasten off and weave in yarn ends.

BOX

Hold lid upside down, join Bright Green to first st of Rnd 6 with slst 1 (does not count as a st). Start next rnd in same st (see Photo 6).

Rnds 1 and 2 (2 rnds): sc 1 in each st. (32 sts)

Rnds 3 and 4 (2 rnds): change to Red, sc 1 in each st.

Rnds 5 and 6 (2 rnds): change to Bright Green, sc 1 in each st.

Rnd 7: work in BLO, [sc 3, sc3tog, sc 2] 4 times. (24 sts)

Rnd 8: [sc 2, sc3tog, sc 1] 4 times. (16 sts)

Stuff firmly.

Rnd 9: [sc 1, sc3tog] 4 times. (8 sts)

Fasten off, sew hole closed by pulling yarn tail through front loops of remaining sts.

Using White, embroider vertical and horizontal lines on sides of box to create tartan-like pattern.

RIBBON

Row 1: using Mustard, ch 100. (100 chs)

Fasten off.

Wrap ribbon around gift box making a bow at top.

Stitch Guide

DIFFERENCE BETWEEN V AND X SINGLE CROCHET (SC)

There are two ways to work a single crochet stitch: the classic V-shape and the X-shape, also known as cross stitch single crochet. The characters in this book are worked with X-shape sc, but they could be worked with V-shape sc instead, as long as you consider the difference in the final result.

CLASSIC V-SHAPE

Insert hook in st, yarn over **(A)**, pull yarn through st, yarn over, draw through both loops on hook.

This creates a V-shape on the front of the stitch **(B)**.

X-SHAPE

Insert hook in st, yarn under **(C)**, pull yarn through st, yarn over, draw through both loops on hook.

This creates a X-shape on the front of the stitch **(D)**.

The X-shape sc creates a tighter, smaller stitch, a denser fabric and smaller amigurumi. The V-shape sc creates a more elastic and fluid fabric.

The stitch torsion is also different (how stitches shift when worked in a continuous spiral). The V-shape sc creates a noticeable diagonal drift **(B)**, whereas X-shape sc are more vertically aligned **(D)**. Some projects have multiple color changes within a round to create vertical stripes or facial features: X-shape sc will keep stitch torsion to a minimum to maintain the integrity of the colorwork.

WORKING IN BACK BUMP OF A CHAIN

The front of the foundation chain has a sequence of "V"s **(E)**; the back has a row of bars often referred to as back bumps, back bars, or third loop **(F)**. Working in the back bump of a chain will give a neat edge to both sides of the chain, which is useful when working around the foundation chain (see: Crocheting Around Foundation Chain).

WORKING IN ROUNDS

The characters and accessories in this book are mostly worked with the amigurumi method, in a continuous spiral without closing rounds. Stitch markers are important to keep track of your rounds. A few pieces are worked in closed rounds, which will be specified in each pattern.

CROCHETING AROUND FOUNDATION CHAIN

Some pieces start with an oval shape.

1. Make a foundation chain as given in pattern, work first set of sts in back bump of chain (see: Working in Back bump of a Chain) **(G)**.

2. Work half of last group of sts to be worked in last back bump in back bump.

3. Turn foundation chain and work remaining sts to be worked in last back bump through "V" of chain stitches **(H)**.

4. Work 2nd set of sts through "V" of chains to complete round **(I)**.

You can work around a foundation chain by working the first set of stitches through the back loops and the 2nd set through the front loops, but this will leave holes between the sides of the first round.

INCREASE (INC)

An increase is two single crochet stitches worked in the same stitch to grow the size of your work.

DECREASE (DEC)

This involves working stitches together to reduce the size. I used the invisible single crochet decrease because it is less noticeable.

INVISIBLE SINGLE CROCHET DECREASE

1. Insert hook under front loop of first st and under front loop of 2nd st **(J)**.

2. Yarn under (or yarn over if working in V-shape sc), pull yarn through both front loops **(K)**.

3. Yarn over, draw through both loops on hook to complete decrease **(L)**.

CHANGING COLOR

Introduce the new color in the final yarn over of the last stitch of the previous color. This will leave the new color on your hook ready to work the next stitch **(A)**.

STRAIGHT STRIPE COLOR CHANGE

To highlight garments this technique creates a straight edge when changing color from one round to next.

1. Following instruction in pattern, work a round of slsts with new color, then in 2nd round insert hook through back loops of slip stitches and both loops of last round of previous color **(B)**.

2. This creates a neat edge of unworked loops to be used later for hems and cuffs.

JOINING YARN TO ADD A DETAIL

Some details are worked directly onto another piece using unworked loops (or stitches) strategically placed.

Hold the piece as mentioned (varies depending on pattern), and with a slip knot on your hook insert the hook in the loop/stitch mentioned to join and then work the sequence of stitches in the pattern **(C)**.

INVISIBLE FASTEN OFF

This is used to avoid the "step" at the end of working in a continuous spiral. It will be mentioned when working flat pieces (such as cheeks) but can also be applied to any open piece.

1. Complete last st of round, cut yarn and pull loop on hook out. Thread yarn tail into a tapestry needle, insert needle underneath top "V" of 2nd st, from front to back **(D)**.

2. Insert needle through center of top "V" of last st of round and pull yarn through **(E)**.

3. This creates a false st to mimic the one underneath, correcting the "step" **(F)**.

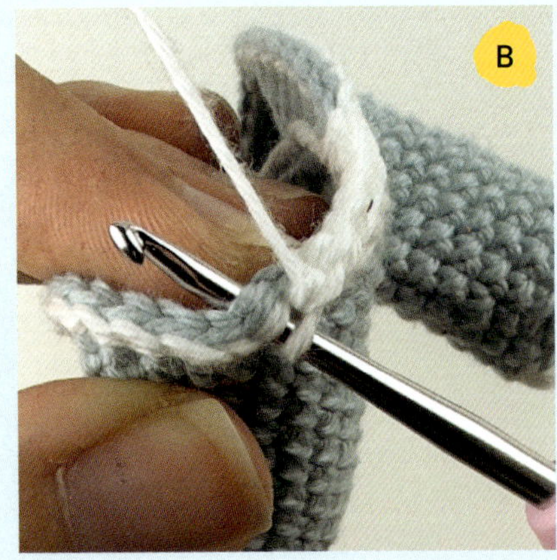

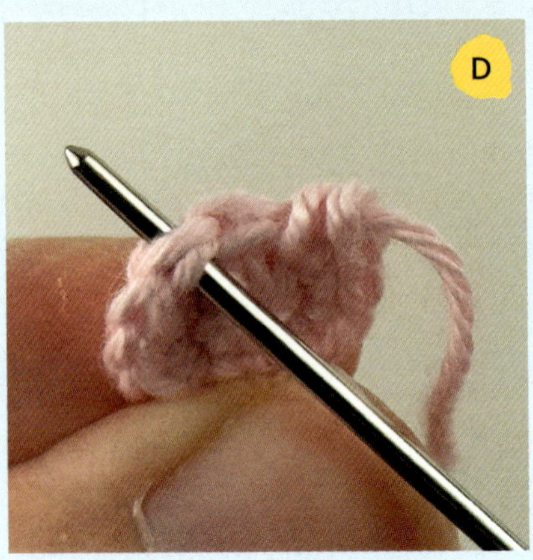

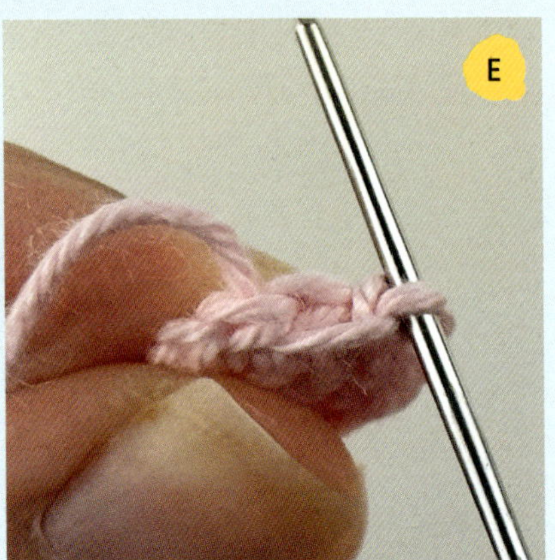

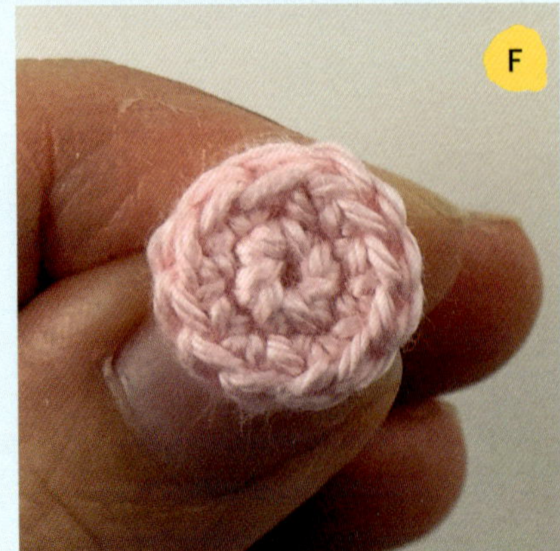

CLOSING WITH SINGLE CROCHET

Some pieces, such as arms, are closed by working single crochet stitches (or other stitches when mentioned) through both layers.

1. Flatten last round of piece so sts on both sides are aligned, insert hook through first pair of sts (st facing you and st facing away) **(G)**, work st through both.

2. Work all pairs of sts until piece is closed. If an odd number of sts, last st of round before closing will be left unworked.

JOINING LEGS

Some characters stand up, so you will need to join the legs to continue with the body.

1. Make first leg as pattern, set aside. Make 2nd leg but don't fasten off. With 2nd leg still on hook, chain number of sts as in pattern **(H)**.

2. Join to first leg by working a sc in the st given in pattern **(I)**. This will be new beginning of round to PM.

3. Cont working around first leg, as well as one loop of chs between legs. Cont on 2nd leg, and finally remaining loop on other side of ch between legs **(J)**.

JOINING FRONT LEGS

Some characters are sitting down, so you will need to join the front legs halfway through the body before continuing.

1. Make front legs as in the pattern, set aside. Make body until front legs are required. With body still on hook, join to first front leg **(K)**.

2. Work number sts as pattern, then skip remaining sts of front leg and same number of sts of body, before working in next st of body as pattern **(L)**.

3. Add 2nd front leg in same way, leaving opening between front legs and body.

4. To close opening, thread yarn tail in tapestry needle and sew front loops of remaining sts of front leg and body. Front legs are now joined and openings closed, so cont working on body and sts made when joining front legs.

ATTACHING YARN STRANDS

1. To attach yarn strands to add detail or texture, insert hook under a st as in pattern, grab strand of yarn in middle and pull a loop through st **(A)**.

2. Grab ends of strand and pull through loop on hook. Pull tightly on strands to secure.

MAKING DOLL GLASSES

You can create doll glasses with craft wire that will fit your amigurumi specifically, or you can also find ready-made doll glasses in notion (haberdashery) stores.

1. Find a plastic tube with diameter of glasses lens. Wrap wire around tube creating a full circle for first lens **(B)**.

2. Bend wire away where it meets for bridge of glasses. Leave a length of straight wire for bridge, long enough to fit spacing between eyes of amigurumi.

3. Wrap wire around tube again for 2nd lens. Cut wire and use pliers if necessary to adjust the curves **(C)**.

Special crochet stitches

Special stitches are used in some of the patterns to add fun textures and details to the characters and their accessories.

PUFF STITCH (PUFF ST)

The number of half double crochet stitches to work for the puff is mentioned in the pattern (for example, 3-hdc puff).

1. Yarn over, insert hook in st as in pattern, yarn over, pull loop through st (three loops on hook) **(D)**.

2. Rep Steps 1 and 2 in same st for number of sts as in pattern (so if making 3-hdc puff, you will have seven loops on hook) **(E)**.

3. Yarn over, draw yarn through all loops on hook to complete puff st **(F)**.

A

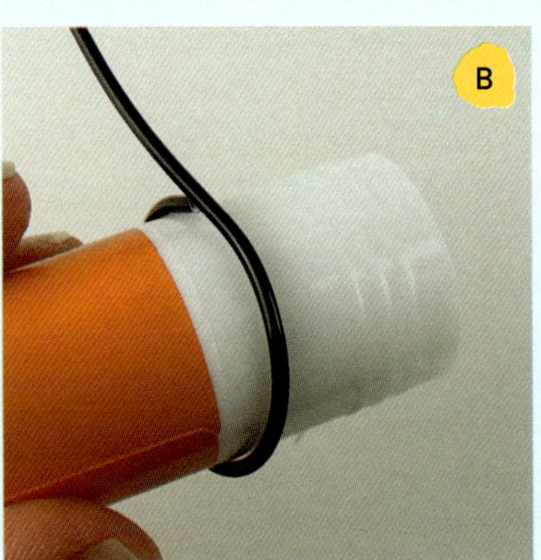
B

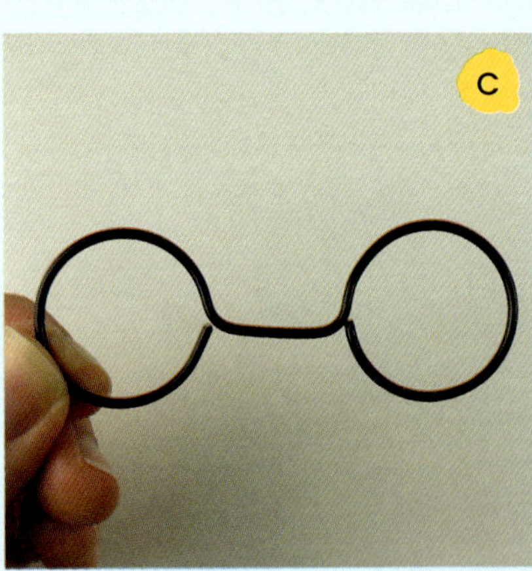
C

D

E

F

BOBBLE STITCH (BOBBLE)

The number of double crochet stitches to work for the bobble is mentioned in the pattern (for example, 3-dc bobble).

1. Yarn over, insert hook in st as in pattern, yarn over, pull loop through st (three loops on your hook).

2. Yarn over, draw yarn through first two loops on hook (two loops on your hook) **(G)**.

3. Rep Steps 1 and 2 in same st for number of sts as in pattern (so if making 3-dc bobble, you will have four loops on hook) **(H)**.

4. Yarn over, draw yarn through all loops on hook to complete bobble st **(I)**.

SPIKE SINGLE CROCHET (SPIKE SC)

Instead of working in the two loops of the next stitch, the spike stitch is worked in the corresponding stitch one round below.

1. Insert hook in st one round below **(J)**.

2. Yarn over, pull loop through st bringing both loops on hook to same height **(K)**.

3. Yarn over, draw yarn through both loops on hook to complete spike sc **(L)**.

PICOT STITCH (PICOT)

1. Make 3 ch sts.

2. Slst 1 in first ch to complete picot st **(A)**.

FRONT POST DOUBLE CROCHET (FPDC)

The front post double crochet is worked around the stitch (or post) of the next stitch to create a raised texture.

1. Yarn over, insert hook from front to back around next st post **(B)**.

2. Yarn over, pull loop from around st post.

3. Yarn over, draw yarn through first two loops on hook.

4. Yarn over, draw yarn through remaining two loops on hook to complete front post double crochet **(C)**.

5. Rep Steps 1 to 4 for each FPdc in pattern.

SURFACE SLIP STITCH (SURFACE SLST)

Surface crochet is worked through the fabric leaving stitches on the surface, instead of working through the top of stitches.

1. Insert hook through fabric from front to back where you want to start working surface sts, holding yarn at back of fabric, pull a loop of yarn up through fabric **(D)**.

2. Insert hook in next st/space **(E)**.

3. With working yarn still at back of fabric, yarn over, draw yarn up through fabric and loop on hook to complete surface slst **(F)**.

4. Rep Steps 2 and 3 as many times as required.

Embroidery

Some embroidery is required for embellishments or facial features.

FRENCH KNOT

1. Thread yarn (or embroidery floss/thread) into a yarn needle, insert needle from back to front where you want to make French knot **(G)**.

2. Wrap yarn twice around needle **(H)**.

3. Insert needle back through fabric close to where yarn came out on Step 1 (but not in same hole or knot will unravel) **(I)**.

4. Gently pull needle and yarn through wrapped loops to complete French knot **(J)**.

STRAIGHT STITCH

1. Thread yarn (or embroidery floss) into yarn needle, insert needle from back to front where you want straight stitch to begin **(K)**.

2. Insert needle back through fabric where you want straight stitch to end **(L)**.

3. Rep Steps 1 and 2 as many times as required. Straight stitches can be worked in any direction, not just in a straight line.

About the author

Hello! I am Andreia and I live in Portugal with my husband Maurício and our two pets Sunny (a little mutt dog) and Moony (a spooky black cat).

My crochet journey started in 2015, watching YouTube tutorials to learn as much as I could, and after I finished my first amigurumi (a wonky panda) I never stopped.

Creating my characters with fun stories helps me give shape to my creativity. When I'm not crocheting I enjoy baking delicious desserts and reading fantasy and mystery novels.

Throughout this last decade, I've been able to do what I love while also collaborating with yarn companies, and I have had my work featured in magazines such as *Simply Crochet*, *Crochet Now*, and *Molliemakes*, and in the *Zoomigurumi book series.*

I hope you enjoy this collection of amigurumi friends and I can't wait to see your makes!

Instagram @lemonyarncreations

Suppliers

Yarn brand: Hobbii

Website: www.hobbii.com

Acknowledgments

First and foremost, I would like to thank my husband, Maurício, for always supporting me and cooking delicious meals to keep me going.

To my parents, even though this was not the path they imagined for me, they saw the joy crochet brings into my life and let me go for it.

To the David and Charles team, thank you for believing in me and this project. Writing a book has been a dream of mine for many years, and I couldn't have done it without your help.

To my crochet friend Lex, thank you for the late-night hangouts on Teams, and for exchanging words of advice, while going through the same journey of writing a book about amigurumi. And to the lovely people from the crochet community, for their encouragement that fuels this passion every day.

A big thank you to my Patreon supporters. Without them, the start of this collection would have remained just an idea for a lot longer. And of course, thank you to my amazing pattern testers: Dorien, Emily, Timber, Catarina, Jess J., Anne-Laure, Ivy, Jess D., Karin, Alicia, Patrícia, Lauren, Heather, Amandine, Jillian, Victoria, Rocio, Kimberly, Nina, Solenne, Marie Florence.

A special thank you to you, the readers, for seeing something in this book that made you want to get to know my characters and have a year filled with Amigurumi friends!

Index

A DAVID AND CHARLES BOOK
© David and Charles, Ltd 2025

David and Charles is an imprint of David and Charles, Ltd, Suite A, Tourism House, Pynes Hill, Exeter, EX2 5WS

Text and Designs © Andreia Ferreira 2025
Layout and Photography © David and Charles, Ltd 2025

First published in the UK and USA in 2025

Andreia Ferreira has asserted her right to be identified as author of this work in accordance with the Copyright, Designs and Patents Act, 1988.

All rights reserved. No part of this publication may be reproduced in any form or by any means, electronic or mechanical, by photocopying, recording or otherwise, without prior permission in writing from the publisher.

No part of this publication may be used or reproduced in any manner for the purpose of training artificial intelligence technologies or systems without permission from David and Charles Ltd.

Readers are permitted to reproduce any of the designs in this book for their personal use and without the prior permission of the publisher. However, the designs in this book are copyright and must not be reproduced for resale.

The author and publisher have made every effort to ensure that all the instructions in the book are accurate and safe, and therefore cannot accept liability for any resulting injury, damage or loss to persons or property, however it may arise.

Names of manufacturers and product ranges are provided for the information of readers, with no intention to infringe copyright or trademarks.

A catalogue record for this book is available from the British Library.

ISBN-13: 9781446314913 paperback
ISBN-13: 9781446314944 EPUB

This book has been printed on paper from approved suppliers and made from pulp from sustainable sources.

Printed in Turkey through Omur Printing & Packaging for:
David and Charles, Ltd, Suite A, Tourism House, Pynes Hill, Exeter, EX2 5WS

10 9 8 7 6 5 4 3 2

Publishing Director: Ame Verso
Senior Commissioning Editor: Sarah Callard
Publishing Manager: Jeni Chown
Editor: Jessica Cropper
Tech Editor: Lauren Willis
Project Editor: Marie Clayton
Designer: Jess Pearson
Pre-press Designer: Susan Reansbury
Illustrations and Art Direction: Jess Pearson
Photography: Jason Jenkins
Production Manager: Beverley Richardson

David and Charles publishes high-quality books on a wide range of subjects. For more information visit **www.davidandcharles.com.**

Share your makes with us on social media using **#dandcbooks** and follow us on Facebook and Instagram by searching for **@dandcbooks.**

Layout of the digital edition of this book may vary depending on reader hardware and display settings.